Baksheesh or Bribe: Cultural Conventions and Legal Pitfalls

A Primer on the Foreign Corrupt Practices Act

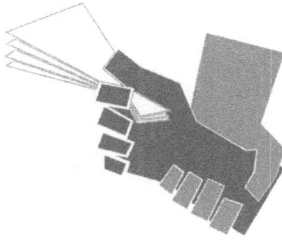

Frank J. Cavico and **Bahaudin G. Mujtaba**

ILEAD Academy, LLC
Davie, Florida. United States of America
www.ileadacademy.com

Frank J. Cavico and Bahaudin G. Mujtaba, 2011. *Baksheesh or Bribe: Cultural Conventions and Legal Pitfalls.*

Cover Design by: Cagri Tanyar

ISBN-13: 978-1-936237-04-3

ISBN-10: 1-936237-04-0

Subject Code & Description
    BUS008000 - Business & Economics: Business Ethics
    LAW051000 - Law: International
    BUS010000 - Business & Economics: Business Law
    PHI005000 - Philosophy: Ethics & Moral Philosophy

Printed in the United States of America by ILEAD Academy, LLC. Davie, Florida.

☆ International ☆
ILEAD ACADEMY
Leadership Education and Associate Development Academy

Table of Contents

Preface

Globalization of the economy is accelerating, international competition is increasing, and U.S. businesses, and not just "big business," are venturing into foreign markets; and consequently are encountering often very challenging multi-cultural business environments. One aspect of "going global" is the presence of complex anti-corruption laws that create potentially very serious legal risks; and thus warrant the keen consideration of the international business executive, manager, and/or entrepreneur. This book primarily addresses one major anti-corruption statute – the United States Foreign Corrupt Practices Act (FCPA). The book also examines other foreign anti-corruption laws as well as international agreements. A fundamental purpose of this book is to raise awareness of the FCPA in the business community and to demonstrate that the FCPA is a very generally and very vaguely written statute as well as one without the benefit of precise judicial interpretation or regulatory guidance. Moreover, the FCPA is a statute with very serious legal consequences; and is a law that in recent years has been very aggressively enforced by the U.S. Department of Justice and Securities and Exchange Commission. Accordingly, the authors examine this important statute, focusing on its anti-bribery provisions and their legal implications for global executives, managers, entrepreneurs, and their companies. Then the authors provide strategies and tactics for the international business person to avoid legal liability under the FCPA. Officials around the world have provided "best practices" to create awareness of laws that apply to bribery. For example, the depiction of the clasped hands and money on the cover to this book represents part of an actual anti-corruption and anti-bribery campaign in Russia[1].

The authors also examine bribery in a variety of cultural contexts and from certain ethical perspectives. A case study is presented based on a noteworthy actual bribery prosecution by the U.S. Department of Justice along with several case discussion questions. The case study serves to raise important legal and ethical issues and to demonstrate significant legal principles as well as to show the complexity, yet also ambiguity, of this area of the law. Finally, the authors provide a series of short case problems of typical bribery scenarios, which can be used for legal analysis, discussion, and training purposes. The book is intended for use as a supplementary academic text in international

---

[1] *Special thanks go to Dr. Yuliya Yurova, Nova Southeastern University, for her translation of the Russian anti-bribery sign - website: http://urbanspotlight.wordpress.com/2009/07/15/hello-world/*

business and management courses and business law and government regulation of business courses as well as a resource for corporate training purposes.

The authors hope that all the aforementioned goals and purposes of this book are achieved in a stimulating, thought-provoking, and perhaps at times provocative, and enjoyable manner; and as a result we hope that the knowledge of the reader is increased, the mental acuity of the reader is enhanced, and the mental discipline of the reader is strengthened. For more detailed information on relevant topics, readers can refer to other books written by the authors, which are as follows:

1. Cavico, F. J., Mujtaba, B. G., and McFarlane, D. (2010). *The State of Business Schools: Educational and Moral Imperatives for Market Leaders.* ILEAD Academy: Davie, Florida.

2. Cavico, F. J. and Mujtaba, B. G. (2009). *Business Ethics: The Moral Foundation of Leadership, Management, and Entrepreneurship (2nd edition).* Pearson Custom Publications: Boston, United States.

3. _____ (2008). *Legal Challenges for the Global Manager and Entrepreneur.* Kendall-Hunt Publishing Company: United States.

4. _____ (2008). *Business Law for the Entrepreneur and Manager.* ILEAD Academy: Davie, Florida, USA.

5. Mujtaba, B. G. and Cavico, F. J. (2010). *The Aging Workforce: Challenges and Opportunities for Human Resource Professionals.* ILEAD Academy: Davie, Florida.

Finally, the authors want you, the readers, to know that they have created a scholarship at their school, The H. Wayne Huizenga School of Business and Entrepreneurship, Nova Southeastern University, called the *Business Ethics and Global Corporate Social Responsibility Fund*, to which they donate a material portion of their royalties from the sale of all their books.

Frank and Bahaudin

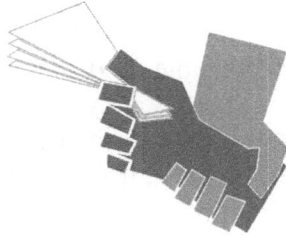

CHAPTER ONE

Introduction to Bribery

Bribery is often seen as a way of "merely" "speeding up the process" or "navigating the system" and thus "getting things done" in an efficient and effective manner. Yet bribery can have more consequential and deleterious ramifications. This introductory chapter discusses bribery, defines it, and provides some basic content pertaining to corruption generally and to types of bribes specifically. The chapter also provides information as to the recent sharp increase in bribery investigations and prosecutions by the United States government.

Introduction

Is the payment to the foreign government official merely "baksheesh" (in Persian) or a bribe? Is it a culturally appropriate gift or tip or a criminal felony? For years now, business schools have been inculcating the values of cultural awareness, sensitivity, maturity, and competency; and corporate training programs have reinforced these values. Yet schools of business as well as corporate training programs also rightly and strongly emphasize the values of legality and morality. So what exactly is this payment to the foreign official? Is it a legal, moral, socially responsible, and culturally acceptable "little" gift, or is it an illegal, immoral, socially irresponsible, and culturally inappropriate "big" crime of bribery? The purposes of this book are to seek answers to these questions with the focus centered on a major law of the United States that prohibits the bribery of foreign officials – the Foreign Corrupt Practices Act (FCPA). This important statute is a 1977 law that prohibits U.S. companies from paying or offering to pay anything of value to foreign government officials or employees of state-owned enterprises in order to retain or obtain business or to secure a competitive advantage. This book will examine this important statute and will seek to explain its major provisions. The accounting provisions of the statute as well as its anti-bribery provisions will be explicated, with particular attention being paid to the bribery provisions. The elements of an illegal bribe will be explicated. A significant exception in the law and the two principal affirmative defenses to liability also will be discussed.

In addition to the FCPA, other global anti-corruption and anti-bribery efforts will be discussed. The book will also discuss how companies can avoid or lessen the risk of legal liability pursuant to the FCPA, in particular by the creation of effective FCPA compliance programs. Whistleblowing in the context of bribery will also be addressed. Legal as well as practical recommendations will be offered to the global executive, manager, and entrepreneur in order to mitigate the risks of legal liability. Public affairs and public relations strategies also will be offered. A case study of an actual bribery legal case that well illustrates many of the pertinent legal and ethical principles and practical points will be provided. The case includes a series of discussion questions that the authors hope will elicit thought-provoking analysis and discussion. The authors will also provide an examination of bribery in the context of culture and cultural conventions, and will address the morality of bribery pursuant to ethics, principally the theory of Ethical Relativism. Finally, a section of Case Problems with scenarios of "payments" to foreign officials is provided for analysis, discussion, and training purposes.

Background and Overview

Today, the economy is truly a global one; accordingly, businesses, and not just giant multinational ones, operate in foreign host countries where the laws, practices, standards, and levels of development are at times much different from a firm's home country. Bribery and corruption too are global phenomena which plague rich, industrialized nations as well as poor developing ones. Even advanced economies have to be vigilant to the dangers of corruption. The term "corruption" is a broad one, generally meaning any misuse of entrusted power – in the private as well as public sector. Bribery, the focal point of this work, is "merely" one form of corruption, though one with a coercive element. Other forms are embezzlement, theft, fraud, extortion, nepotism, favoritism, and conflict of interest. Generally, bribery is the granting of some type of benefit in order to unduly influence an action or decision. Bribery can be initiated by the person wanting some type of preferential treatment or by the person who seeks or solicits the payment. Bribery can be called "aggressive" or "active," where the bribe-giver desires some type of affirmative action, or "defensive" or "passive," where the bribe-giver wants something overlooked or protected. Bribery can also be called "grand" and "petty." "Grand" bribes arise where large sums of money typically are given to government officials in order to secure a contract. These bribes, according to Weinograd (2010), "are typically larger in size, corrupt in purpose, and paid to achieve an end not natural to the ordinary operations of government apparatus" (p. 517). A "petty" bribe occurs where the sums are smaller, but the payment is usually more frequent, and characteristically involves lower level and local government officials. These latter payments are at times referred to as "transaction bribes," or "grease" or "speed money," to expedite and facilitate access to and performance of routine government services. As explained by Weinograd (2010), the purpose of such "grease" is "merely to lubricate the wheels that bureaucratic friction would otherwise grind to a halt" (p. 517). Bribes, finally, can be characterized as "purchase" or "variance" bribes. In the former a payment is made to the foreign official with a corrupt motive to induce the foreign official to misuse his or her position or authority in order to wrongfully secure a contract or direct business to one's firm. A "variance" bribe is one in which the corrupt motive is to induce the foreign official to wrongfully exempt one's firm from the host country's law, for example, a payment to suspend the local pollution regulations from being enforced against one's firm. This work will focus on "purchase" bribes.

Recently, there have been many news reports of bribery, bribery investigations, and bribery prosecutions, particularly by the U.S. government. Legal commentators have noted that "although the FCPA has historically generated relatively few actions, there has been a recent flurry of investigations and self-disclosures regarding FCPA" (Bishop and Johnson, 2009, p. 25). One legal commentator declared that the recent enforcement of the FCPA by the U.S. Justice Department (DOJ) and the Securities and Exchange Commission (SEC) has been "exponential" (Thomas, 2010, p. 439). Lindsey (2009) states that the DOJ and the SEC "have increased their enforcement of the FCPA in the past seven years. Since 2002 the DOJ and SEC have initiated 69 FCPA matters against corporations and individuals, a marked increase in the number of prosecutions between 1977, when the law was enacted, and 2002. Recently, fines and penalties have reached record levels" (p. 960). Dworsky (2009) states that "U.S. regulatory authorities have recently more aggressively enforced the FCPA, expanding jurisdictional reach and exacting higher penalties" (pp. 696-97). Thomas (2010) reports that the number of bribery prosecutions pursuant to the FCPA brought between 2001 and 2006 was more than four times that of the previous five years; and that the number had doubled in 2007 from 2006 (p. 449).

The most recent bribery investigation as of the writing of this book, as reported by the *Wall Street Journal* (Crawford and Searcy, 2010), involves Hewlett-Packard Company (H-P) and allegations that the company executives paid millions of dollars in bribes to Russian government officials in order for the company to secure contracts. The U.S. Justice Department is investigating the company to see if it violated the Foreign Corrupt Practices Act. The investigation is seeking to determine if H-P executives paid almost $11 million in bribes in order to obtain a 35 million Euro contract to supply computer equipment throughout Russia. The government is investigating whether H-P executives devised a scheme to transmit money to Russia by means of a complex network of German operatives, shell companies ranging from Wyoming to New Zealand, and a Moscow computer supplier. In particular, the investigation is focusing on a German H-P subsidiary, which received the payment for the contract but then allegedly paid the bribes back to Russian government officials. The Russian government officials have not yet been identified. The *Wall Street Journal* also reported that the German government is conducting an investigation.

To illustrate further, the *Wall Street Journal* reported in 2009 that the U.S. Justice Department has been steadily increasing its prosecutions of foreign bribery misconduct by U.S. corporations, noting that as of May 2009 "at least" 120 companies were being investigated for violations of the Foreign Corrupt Practices Act (Searcy, 2009, p. A1). In April of 2010, the *Wall Street Journal* (Byron, 2010) reported that there were about 150 FCPA investigations under way, according to a Justice Department spokesperson; and that in 2009 the Justice Department brought 34 enforcement actions, which number increased from 17 the year before. Specifically, in 2010, the *Wall Street Journal* (Fuhrmans and Catan, 2010) reported that Daimler AG agreed to settle a bribery investigation instituted by the U.S. Justice Department and the Securities and Exchange Commission (SEC) that alleged that the German company paid tens of millions of dollars to secure business in 22 countries, including China and Russia. Daimler AG not only paid $185 million to settle the case, but also its German and Russian units agreed to plead guilty to violating the Foreign Corrupt Practices Act. The agreement by Daimler to pay as well as the guilty pleas ended the Justice Department's criminal investigation as well as the SEC's related civil investigation. The government had accused Daimler of engaging in a decades-long practice of paying bribes, some as recently as 2008, to foreign government officials through a network of more than 200 off-shore accounts and other secret funds (Fuhrmans and Catan, 2010). The settlement also calls for Daimler to enter a deferred prosecution agreement whereby the Justice Department will not prosecute the company if it continues to cooperate with regulators and adheres to internal controls to combat corruption and bribery (Fuhrmans and Catan, 2010). The *Wall Street Journal* further reported that from 2006-2009, the Criminal Division of the Justice Department had instituted 58 cases pursuant to the FCPA (Searcy, 2009). The *Wall Street Journal* (Searcy, 2009) reported in 2009 that the Justice Department indicted six former employees of Control Components, Inc., which makes energy equipment and valves for energy facilities, for making allegedly 236 allegedly improper payments totaling almost $5 million, from 2003 to 2007, in order to obtain contracts in more than thirty countries, including China and Malaysia (Searcy, 2009).

In 2008, the *Wall Street Journal* had already reported a "global crackdown" against companies that use bribery to advance their business interests internationally, including "dramatically increased" investigations and prosecutions (Gold and Crawford, 2008, p. B1). The newspaper reported that the German engineering conglomerate, Siemens AG, agreed to pay an $800 million fine to the U.S. government, which fine was the largest penalty ever imposed under the FCPA, to end claims filed by the Justice Department that the company had spent more than $1 billion in recent years bribing government officials in at least 10 countries to obtain a wide variety of contracts, from building refineries, supplying power, and providing medical equipment (Fuhrmans, 2009). One of the officials who allegedly was bribed by Siemens was the former president of Argentina (Esterl and Crawford, 2008). The *Wall Street Journal* quoted government court filings, which stated the bribery by the company was "systemic" and involved "employees at all levels of the company, including former senior management" (Esterl and Crawford, 2008, p. B1). The newspaper also cited the recent conviction of a former Halliburton executive who led a scheme to bribe Nigerian officials to obtain lucrative contracts related to the natural gas business. The executive, who was the chairman of the Halliburton subsidiary, Kellogg, Brown, & Root, received a seven year prison sentence, which was as the writing of this book the longest sentence imposed pursuant to the Foreign Corrupt Practices Act (FCPA) (Gold and Crawford, 2008; Gold, 2008). Halliburton Company also agreed to pay $559 million to the United States to settle charges that one of its former units had bribed Nigerian officials during the construction of a gas plant. The payment was at the time the largest sum ever paid by a U.S. company to settle a bribery investigation. The construction of the gas plant in Nigeria was at the time the largest industrial investment ever made in Africa (Gold, 2009). The *Wall Street Journal* (Eaton, 2008) also reported in 2008 that the Willbros Group, Inc., which is a Houston-based oil services company, agreed to pay $32.3 million in criminal and civil fines to settle allegations that it bribed government officials in Nigeria to obtain contracts. Company officials of the firm's international subsidiary were accused of agreeing to pay more than $6.3 million in bribes to Nigerian government officials in order to secure and to keep a $387 million contract to construct a gas pipeline project in Nigeria. The *Wall Street Journal* (Eaton, 2008) also noted that two former employees of the company have pleaded guilty to charges related to the case. The *Wall Street Journal*, furthermore, reported that in 2007 a subsidiary of the Houston-based oil-field services company, Baker Hughes, Inc., pleaded guilty to violating the FCPA, and agreed to pay $44 million in fines for bribing government officials in Kazakhstan to obtain oil-related work (Gold and Crawford, 2008). One legal commentator described all these recent fines as "extraordinary" (Singer, 2009, p. 293).

 To underscore how aggressive the U.S. government has now become in enforcing the FCPA, the authors would point to a *Sun-Sentinel* (McMahon, 2010) article in 2010 that reported on a government bribery "sting" in Broward County, Florida, where 22 employees, including CEOs and workers, of military and law enforcement supply companies, were arrested and charged with conspiring to bribe a high-level foreign government official. Two of the principals in the alleged conspiracy were accused of agreeing to pay a 20% "commission" to a "sales agent" they thought was representing the defense minister of an unidentified African country. The 22 executives and workers, from companies in the U.S., Great Britain, and Israel, were trying to obtain part of a $15 million deal to supply and outfit the African country's presidential guard with equipment, such as body armor and bulletproof vests. The "sales agent" they were dealing with was actually an undercover FBI agent. If convicted, the suspects are looking at maximum sentences of up to 20 years in prison. The *Wall Street Journal* (Perez and Kendall, 2010) also reported on this bribery "sting" story; and quoted an Assistant Attorney General in the Criminal Division of the Justice Department who stated that the sting, which was in operation for two years, should deter bribery by compelling executives involved in potential bribery schemes to ask themselves the following question: "Am I really paying off a foreign government official or is this a federal agent" (p. A3)?

Apparently, even the United Nations is not immune from corruption. The *Sun-Sentinel* (Heilprin, 2010) newspaper reported an Associated Press story in 2010 that the FBI "sting" involving defense contractors and fake salespersons for an African defense minister has now implicated the United Nations, and has uncovered a series of cases of bribes and bid-rigging for multi-million dollar U.N. peace-keeping contracts. What was particularly disturbing about the story was the revelation that the U.N., which spends billions of dollars each year, had an anti-corruption task force, but it was disbanded in 2008 (Heilprin, 2010). One legal commentator related that the recent increase in enforcement actions by the Justice Department was only the "tip of the iceberg" regarding the FCPA (Spalding, 2010, p. 354).

Consequently, there is now plainly a heightened legal risk environment for businesses operating internationally. So why is there this upsurge in anti-corruption and anti-bribery investigations, prosecutions, fines, and convictions? The *Wall Street Journal* (Gold and Crawford, 2008) posited four major reasons for this stepped-up anti-bribery activity. First, cooperation and assistance among the government investigators in different nations have been increasing.

"The U.S. has markedly increased its cooperation with foreign regulators in recent years" (Michaels and Bryan-Low, 2010, p. B6). Second, companies are now voluntarily turning over to government officials the evidence of wrongdoing in the expectation of receiving leniency from prosecutors. Third, the passage of the Sarbanes-Oxley law in the U.S. in 2002, which requires executives to certify that their companies' financial records are complete and accurate, and which imposes harsh penalties for misstatements and non-disclosures. Pursuant to the Sarbanes-Oxley law, a bribe that is misrepresented as a legitimate business expense on the corporate records, for example, as a consultant's fee, could be considered a deceptive entry on the corporation's books, thus triggering the law. Also, the Sarbanes-Oxley Act has provisions protecting whistleblowing employees as well as very harsh penalties for retaliating against whistleblowers. Finally, many companies now have compliance programs to detect and to deter bribery as well as codes of ethics and codes of conduct, which explicitly prohibit bribery, and which are not mere "window-dressing," but rather "policed" and enforceable company rules.

Summary

This introductory chapter discussed bribery, defined it, and provided some basic content pertaining to corruption generally and to types of bribes specifically. The chapter also provided information as to the recent sharp increase in bribery investigations and prosecutions by the United States government. The next chapter will analyze the very important anti-bribery statute in the United States – the Foreign Corrupt Practices Act.

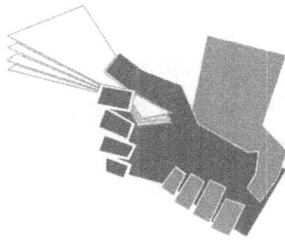

CHAPTER TWO

Legal Analysis of the Foreign Corrupt Practices Act (FCPA)

This chapter analyzes the Foreign Corrupt Practices Act (FCPA), which is a very significant anti-bribery statute in the United States, and one that has global legal and practical ramifications. An overview and historical background will be provided. Then the chapter will examine the two major parts to the statute – the anti-bribery provisions and the accounting provisions, with particular attention focused on the former. The sanctions and penalties that can be imposed for statutory violations will also be addressed.

Introduction

The Foreign Corrupt Practices Act (FCPA) of 1977 has two main parts: 1) an anti-bribery component that makes it illegal to provide anything of value to officials of foreign governments or political parties with the wrongful intent to obtain or retain business; and 2) an accounting component that requires companies to maintain books and records that thoroughly and accurately reflect transactions with foreign officials as well as to establish and maintain appropriate internal controls to ensure the integrity of the records and accounting processes. As stated by Singer (2009), "the purpose of the law was straightforward: to prohibit corporate bribery abroad and encourage rigorous and faithful bookkeeping at home" (p. 274). Weinograd (2010) relates that the unambiguous design of the U.S. Congress in promulgating the FCPA was "to combat the rampant corruption that plagued international commerce and thereby aimed to minimize bribery's corrosive effects on foreign societies and domestic corporate culture" (pp. 510-11). The statute reflects the public policy of the United States that the payment of bribes to foreign government officials in order to secure business was unethical, contrary to the democratic values of the people of the United States, as well as harmful to good governance and the rule of law, contrary to the principles of fair competition, an impediment to economic progress, and thus inimical to society (Dworsky, 2009; Lindsey, 2009). Singer (2009) explains that the two major sections of the statute, though unified in basic purpose,

> ...vary in some conceptually important ways. The books and records section, for instance, is fundamentally prescriptive; it contains an intricate set of accounting and bookkeeping guidelines intended to reduce the likelihood of corruption among complying corporations. In contrast, the anti-bribery component operates proscriptively to punish companies found to have engaged in corrupt activities overseas (p. 278).

Accounting Provisions

The Foreign Corrupt Practices Act has two fundamental requirements: record-keeping and internal controls. The Act requires companies to keep records and accounts in reasonable detail; accordingly, businesses must establish internal accounting systems, processes, and controls in order to provide assurances that transactions are transparent, accurate, executed in accordance with company standards and authorization, and are, of course, legal. The books, records, and accounts of a business must be accurate, and fairly reflect in reasonable detail the transactions made by the company as well as the disposition of its assets. The reason for these accounting provisions is to make it more difficult for companies to hide the source of bribery payments by false accounting entries or in some type of secret foreign bank account or "slush" fund, as well as to otherwise attempt to circumvent the law by hiding, falsifying, or misrepresenting payments or transactions. It is important to note that the accounting provisions only apply to publicly traded companies, and thus the FCPA's accounting and record-keeping provisions are found in the Securities and Exchange Act of 1934 (Bishop and Johnson, 2009). Pursuant to SEC standards, criminal liability under the FCPA can only be imposed for the knowing falsification of books and records, the knowing circumvention of accounting controls, or the knowing failure to implement the required internal accounting systems and controls (Bishop and Johnson, 2009; Dworsky, 2009). The Securities and Exchange Commission is primarily responsible for enforcing the books and records provisions of the FCPA (Singer, 2009).

Anti-Bribery Provisions

The Foreign Corrupt Practices Act makes bribery illegal when seven basic requirements are met: 1) the use of a means or an instrumentality of interstate commerce; 2) in furtherance of a payment or transfer of anything of value, or offer to pay or transfer, directly or indirectly; 3) to any foreign government official with discretionary authority (or any foreign political party or candidate or political party official); 4) when the purpose of the payment is "corrupt," that is, intended to get the foreign official from acting or not acting; 5) with knowledge that the payment or something of value would be passed on to the foreign official or other parties; 6) for the purpose of influencing an official act or decision; 7) in order to assist the company in obtaining, retaining, or directing business for or with any person or business (Thomas, 2010; Weinograd, 2010; Dworsky, 2009; Singer, 2009). These legal provisions are also applicable to payments made to officials of public international organizations, such as the United Nations or World Trade Organization (Thomas, 2010; Bishop and Johnson, 2009).

Technically, the FCPA applies to "domestic concerns" and "issuers" as well as any person who authorizes or commits a violation while in the territory of the United States. "Domestic concerns" encompass U.S. citizens or residents wherever located as well as any corporation, partnership, organization, including sole proprietorships, that is formed pursuant to the laws of the United States or which have their principal place of business in the United States. "Issuers" encompass companies that trade their shares on a U.S. stock exchange as well as foreign companies that sell American Depository Receipts on U.S. exchanges. The fact that the statute applies to any company that lists its shares on U.S. exchanges gives the Justice Department a wide grant of jurisdictional authority to reach the payments by companies, even foreign ones, overseas. The FCPA also applies to officers, directors, and employees of an "issuer" or "domestic concern," even if these individuals are not U.S. citizens (Lindsey, 2009). Dworsky (2009) points out that the anti-bribery provisions of the FCPA are much broader than the accounting provisions, since the latter apply only to "issuers" but the former apply to "any person." The expansion of the anti-bribery provisions to "any person" was the result of the amendment to the FCPA in 1998 (Dworsky, 2009). The 1998 amendments also removed the requirement of a territorial connection between the corrupt act and the United States; that is, the "FCPA can reach foreign agents and employees of domestic concerns, and U.S. nationals living anywhere in the world who have very little contact with the United States" (Dworsky, 2009, p. 682).

The U.S. government, moreover, takes a very broad view of each element in the statute. Singer (2009) relates that "the anti-bribery component of the FCPA casts a wider jurisdictional net than its recordkeeping counterpart" (p. 279). For example, regarding the requirement of obtaining or retaining business, paying bribes to secure a contract would, of course, trigger the statute; but Lindsey (2009) relates that a violation can also occur if a company obtained some type of "improper business advantage" from the payment to the foreign government official, for example, reducing custom duties and waiving regulations, even if no specific contract was secured (Lindsey, 2009, p. 963). To illustrate, in the case of *United States v. Kay*, two corporate employees admitted bribing Haitian government officials in order to secure favorable but unlawful tax and tariff relief. The corporate defendants contended that these payments were outside the reach of the FCPA since, they argued, the statute only criminalizes payments made for the purpose of securing or maintaining business. The Fifth Circuit Court of Appeals, however, rejected their argument, and ruled that a sufficient business connection to the FCPA was established (Weinograd, 2010). Similarly, the territorial jurisdictional reach of the statute is interpreted broadly in that the government can have jurisdiction over acts that occur outside the U.S., as well as those who authorize such acts, if the acts cause further acts to occur within the United States or its territories (Lindsey, 2000). Dworsky (2009) notes that the "anything of value" language in the statute can encompass both tangible and intangible objects or things, the payment of expenses and consulting fees, charitable donations, and offers of employment. Furthermore, it is not necessary that the money or gift to the foreign official actually exchange hands; rather, the mere offer to pay or to transfer will violate the statute (Lindsey, 2009). "Foreign officials" are also broadly defined. Any person who receives at least a portion of his or her salary from the public treasury of a foreign government will be deemed to be a foreign government official, which includes doctors and nurses who work in state-owned facilities, employees of state-owned companies, as well as government contractors that are working in some type of official government capacity, such as providing security services (Lindsey, 2009).

The "corrupt" requirement is a critical component of the FCPA. As such, the payment must be made with the bad intent or purpose or "evil mind" (called "scienter" under the old common law) to induce the foreign government official to misuse his or her official position and authority in order to wrongfully direct business to one's firm or to obtain some type of undeserved preference or to otherwise accomplish an unlawful end or result (Dworsky, 2009). Legal commentators equate the "corrupt" requirement to a *quid pro quo* whereby "…the United States domestic concern or its agent makes an offer in exchange for a bargain for benefit from a foreign government official" (Bishop and Johnson, 2009, p. 25). The U.S. Court of Appeals has ruled that specific knowledge of FCPA violations is not necessary for liability; rather, all that is necessary is that U.S. business people have the knowledge that bribing foreign officials generally is wrong and illegal, which is, as noted by two legal commentators, part of their "common intelligence" (Bishop and Johnson, 2009, p. 26). Weinograd equates the "corrupt" requirement to a *mens rea* requirement; that is, "Congress intended to criminalize only those payments intentionally designed to induce misuse of foreign officials' authority" (p. 513). This evil motive or purpose is indispensable to liability. However, there is no requirement that the payment violate the law of the host country.

The Foreign Corrupt Practices Act states that it is illegal to transfer something of value to "any person," while "knowing" that the payment or thing of value will be given directly or indirectly to foreign government officials. Since bribe schemes frequently are perpetuated through third party agents, Singer (2009) relates that "acknowledging this, Congress was very careful to lay clear statutory groundwork to discourage U.S. entities from making corrupt payments indirectly" (p. 281). The purpose, therefore, of this "any person" language is to prevent companies from using third party agents to do the transfer, and thus, in essence, to "launder" the bribe through a third party. Further complicating the "knowing" and corrupt motive requirements is the old common law doctrine of vicarious liability, which deals with the imputed legal liability of a principal or employer for the legal wrongs of its agents and employees acting within the course or scope of their duties. However, the mere establishment of an agency relationship is not sufficient to trigger liability, as foreign agents have many very useful and quite legitimate purposes; moreover, even negligent supervision of an agent or employee is not sufficient to trigger criminal liability pursuant to the "knowing" and corrupt motive requirements; however if there is a conscious disregard, willful blindness, or deliberate ignorance by a company of the actions of its agents or employees that violates the FCPA, then the requisite knowing, bad intent, and bad purposes are established (Bishop and Johnson, 2009). If a company is "substantially certain" of a violation, the "knowing" requirement will be satisfied (Dworsky, 2009). Furthermore, a company can be held liable for third party violations if there is an awareness of facts or circumstances that would make such illegal payments highly probable or present a substantial likelihood of their occurrence (Lindsey, 2009). Additionally, reckless conduct or a "firm belief" that a violation was likely to occur will trigger the statute (Singer, 2009). These vicarious liability provisions, according to Singer (2009), are also designed to prevent the circuitous payment of bribes by a subsidiary company on behalf of its parent as well as to motivate parent companies to monitor the conduct of their subsidiaries. The idea is to eliminate the "head-in-the-sand" defense (Singer, 2009). Dworsky (2009) further notes that these vicarious liability provisions apply to actions taken overseas by a company's representatives regardless of their nationality. Spalding (2010) emphasizes that these vicarious liability provisions can cause a "tremendous imbalance between the power of a prosecutor and corporate defendant" since liability may be imposed "even for the most responsible corporate citizen" (p. 405).

To summarize this complex and consequential area of the law, actual or positive knowledge, inferential knowledge, explicit direction or implicit direction, or actual authorization or implicit authorization that a third party intermediary will transfer the illicit payment to the foreign official as a bribe will trigger the FCPA (Spalding, 2010; Lindsey, 2009; Singer, 2009). Dworsky (2009) concludes: "Therefore, simple negligence or mere foolishness should not be sufficient to trigger the Act" (p. 683). The purposes of these direct and vicarious liability provisions are clear, to wit: to prevent the "laundering" of bribes through third parties, to ensure "that management officials could not take refuge from the act's prohibition by their unwarranted obliviousness to any action (inaction), language or other 'signaling device that should reasonably alert them to the 'high probability' of an FCPA violation," (Singer, 2009, p. 289), as well as for companies to ensure they are dealing with reputable third parties and monitoring their conduct.

Yet there is a major exception to liability under the statute; that is, there is the concept of a "legal bribe." The Foreign Corrupt Practices Act recognizes that in many countries government officials, especially lower level ones, expect a little "grease" money, that is relatively small sums to "facilitate and expedite" routine government actions. The 1988 amendments to the FCPA explicitly recognize this exception to bribery; and thus allow payments to secure the performance of the following: obtaining permits, licenses, and other official documents; processing government applications, documents, and other government paper, such as visas; providing police and fire protection; providing mail pick-up and delivery; supplying sanitation services; scheduling inspections; providing telephone service, power, water, and utility services; loading and unloading cargo; getting goods through customs; protecting perishable goods from deterioration; and speeding up the transit of goods across the country (Spalding, 2010; Weinograd, 2010). It is very important to point out that these payments must be made to lower level government officials so that they will perform services that they are legally bound to do; that is, the exception deals with ministerial, "petty bureaucratic," and clerk-like government functions; consequently, the more discretionary authority the government official has the less likely that the paying party will be able to take advantage of this exception. The gist of this legal exception to bribery is that these routine government services would have occurred anyway, but the payments "merely" speed up and make their performance go more smoothly. Yet Weinograd (2010) emphasizes that "routine" is an "expansive" term that has "many connotations, for example, referring to actions "frequently undertaken," actions that are "ordinary," and those that are "widely accepted as legitimate" (p. 515). However, these payments cannot be used to award new business or to maintain business with a particular party (Spalding, 2010; Dworsky, 2009). The exception realistically reflects the "real-world" view that these payments are usually considered normal business practices to afford additional compensation to inadequately compensated lower level government officials. Weinograd (2010) notes that "practitioners, academics, and courts have struggled to delineate facilitating payments from bribes" (p. 514). Furthermore, another legal commentator warns that "this exception is very limited and companies have often made what they consider to be facilitating payments only to discover that the government takes a narrower view (Lindsey, 2009). To illustrate the perplexity of this "routine" exception, Weinograd (2010) asks whether a payment to acquire Internet access in a country where such technology is not commonplace is an illegal bribe or a mere facilitating payment; but Weinograd (2010) does not supply an answer to this "gray area" of the law.

The FCPA also contains two affirmative defenses which were added to the statute by amendments in 1988 (Spalding, 2010; Dworsky, 2009). The first defense arises when the payment to the foreign government official is lawful pursuant to the express written laws, rules, or regulations of the host country. However, the absence of written laws proscribing bribery in the host country would not by itself be sufficient to satisfy this defense (Spalding, 2010; Dworsky, 2009).

The second affirmative defense in the FCPA deals with payments, gifts, or transfers of value to foreign government officials that are directly related to the promotion, demonstration, or explanation of a firm's products or services or the execution or performance of a contract with a country's government or a government agency. These expenditures can cover the travel, lodging, and meals of foreign government officials. In order to be legal, these expenditures must be "reasonable" and *bona fide*. What is "reasonable" depends on several factors, for example, the amounts and costs involved, the occasion, the practices and customs of the country, and the cost and frequency of prior payments or gifts. The burden of proof and persuasion in establishing these affirmative defenses is on the defendant company or individual (Dworsky, 2009).

Penalties

The United States Department of Justice and Securities and Exchange Commission are responsible for enforcing the FCPA. The Department of Justice is solely responsible for criminal enforcement, but may also institute civil proceedings; whereas the Securities and Exchange Commission is responsible for the investigation of 'issuers," that is, publicly traded companies, and can institute civil proceedings; but the agency can also recommend and refer cases to the Justice Department for criminal prosecution (Dworsky, 2009). The penalties for violating the accounting reporting and controls provisions of the FCPA are substantial. For individuals willfully violating the accounting provisions of the statute, the government can impose fines up to $5 million and imprisonment for up to 20 years. For corporations, the maximum fine for violating the accounting provisions is $25 million. The government can impose fines of up to $2 million per violation on companies for violating the anti-bribery provisions of the statute; and can impose a penalty of up to a $100,000 fine as well as up to five years imprisonment for individuals violating the bribery provisions of the law. The government can also impose civil penalties of up to $10,000 per violation on companies and their executives. Additional sanctions imposed on companies are the prohibition from obtaining government contracts; and individuals may be suspended or prohibited from obtaining export licenses or participating in the securities business (Dworsky, 2009). The Justice Department, however, does have an option between prosecuting and not prosecuting, called diversion agreements. Thomas (2010) explains that these diversion agreements take two forms: non-prosecution agreements (NPAs) and deferred prosecution agreements (DPAs). They are used when the government may not want to prosecute, and consequently perhaps destroy a company due to adverse publicity; yet not allow what the government feels is a guilty party to escape justice (Thomas, 2010). Both agreements function as contracts between the DOJ and the potentially guilty parties; if the company completely fulfills the terms of the agreement, the government will not indict or prosecute the company. The agreement typically consists of compliance standards and financial guidelines. The two differ in that a DPA defers the prosecution of an already indicted company, whereas an NPA defers the indictment of a company for a certain period of time. In a DPA, if the agreement is fully complied with the government will dismiss the charges (Thomson, 2010).

Summary

This chapter attempted to delineate some of the major provisions of the FCPA with particular attention being paid to the anti-bribery component to the statute. As one readily has seen, the statute is not very precise, has a broad reach legally and jurisdictionally, and furthermore is broadly interpreted by the U.S. government. Moreover, the law has severe penalties for infractions; and now is being very aggressively enforced by the government. Therefore, the prudent global business person and entrepreneur must be very concerned with this significant U.S. law. However, to further complicate matters for the business person, there are international treaties and other foreign laws to be concerned with, and thus to be cognizant of, in the global business world. These international laws will be discussed in the next chapter.

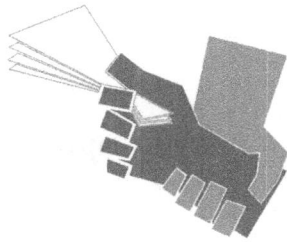

CHAPTER THREE

International Anti-Bribery and Anti-Corruption Laws

This chapter examines important international anti-bribery and anti-corruption laws, with particular attention being focused on the anti-bribery convention of the Organization for Economic Cooperation and Development. Other regional and national anti-bribery and anti-corruption laws are also briefly discussed. Unfortunately, people in public and private sectors of each industry can be involved in corruption. Siddiquee (2010) writes that:

> Although often corruption involves officials holding important positions, one can very well get involved in corruption without holding office in public, private or voluntary organizations. Some examples of corruption which do not necessarily involve public officials include terrorism, smuggling, tax evasion, profiteering, fraud in selling and buying lands, defaulting of bank-loans, under and over-invoicing, currency

manipulation, forgeries, deceit, adulteration of food and medicine, money laundering, and ballot stuffing (pp. 155-156).

Global Anti-Bribery and Anti-Corruption Laws

Global anti-corruption and anti-bribery efforts received a major boost in 1997 with the passage of the anti-bribery convention by the Organization for Economic Cooperation and Development (OECD). In 1998, the FCPA was again amended to implement the OECD convention (Dworsky, 2009). The OECD now has 30 member countries consisting of the world's largest economies and most of the largest trading partners of the United States (Dworsky, 2009; Singer, 2009). The anti-bribery convention was a milestone in the international efforts to legally combat bribery. All member countries have signed the convention as well as seven non-OECD countries (Dworsky, 2009). The OECD convention was the first major global treaty to make the bribery of foreign government officials to obtain business a crime. The agreement sets out criteria for national legislation, some of which is very similar to the FCPA (Singer, 2009) – but the OECD does not mandate specific wording or penalties, and consequently creates a situation where some countries may treat bribery as a far more serious offense than other nations (Sanger, 1997). Moreover, Dworsky (2009) notes that the convention has been criticized because it did not ban outright the tax deductibility of illicit payments and did not criminalize the bribery of political parties and candidates. However, the OECD convention does specifically state that national laws cannot allow a defense often asserted by bribe paying companies and business people that they were "merely" complying with "local customs" when they bribed foreign government officials (Sanger, 1997). The agreement does require the member countries to work with each other to pursue and investigate allegations of bribery. The OECD convention does not include nations outside the OECD, though, as noted, some have signed the anti-bribery convention. In addition, the convention is not uniformly enforced. Nevertheless, due to the convention as well as other international anti-bribery and anti-corruption efforts, Dworsky (2009) recommends that a company should conduct a thorough examination of the laws of the host country, since many countries due to the convention and perhaps changing moral norms, are now likely to have laws prohibiting bribery, whether these laws are enforced is another matter altogether.

Before the OECD treaty, "U.S. businesses were then at a competitive disadvantage in international markets, because foreign competitors were unconstrained by laws prohibiting bribery" (Dworsky, 2009, p. 673). Consequently, prior to the convention, not only was bribery legal in many countries, but also some nations, such as Germany, permitted, and as noted, still may permit, companies to deduct bribes as legitimate business expenses from corporate taxes (Allen, 2000). In Germany, it was illegal to demand and to accept bribes, but not to pay them (Mitchener, 1997). To vividly illustrate the pre-anti-bribery convention environment, consider the laws of France (Buchan, 1997), which did not even have a provision making bribery illegal. However, French law did have a provision making the "misuse of corporate funds" a crime. The Supreme Court of France, in a decision involving the bribery of a government official, a trade minister, to have a tax bill reduced, held that a bribe would not constitute a misuse of corporate funds if the company received something in return. This was the situation in the case at hand since the bribe was effective and the official reduced the tax; and thus there was not a misuse of corporate funds; and the court accordingly ruled no legal wrong. The bribe had worked! The "moral" of this story is that under the pre-convention law, a French business manager or entrepreneur had to have very good judgment and bribe a good, honest, corrupt government official, who will do what he or she is supposed to do in return for the bribe, and not a bad, dishonest, corrupt official, who will take the company's bribe but not do what is expected, thereby causing serious legal "misuse" problems. Confronted by such permissive laws, many U.S. business people argued vociferously that this situation placed them at a distinct competitive disadvantage. One purpose of the OECD, therefore, was to create a level-playing-field for the U.S. international business person. The *New York Times* said the OECD "agreement represents a major victory for American businesses that have long complained that the anti-corruption law passed by Congress (the FCPA)...puts them at a competitive disadvantage around the world" (Sanger, 1997, p. 1).

Yet, how significant this OECD "victory" has been is another matter altogether. One principal problem with this convention is whether other countries consistently and effectively enforce the anti-bribery provisions of the OECD (Dworsky, 2009). However, as more and more countries sign anti-corruption and anti-bribery conventions, as well as promulgate concomitant local laws, and also enforce more consistently and vigorously the laws, the universal standard, contrary to ethical relativism, will be that bribery is illegal and immoral.

Dworsky (2009) discusses four regional anti-bribery and anti-corruption efforts. One was by the Organization of American States, which in 1997 adopted an Inter-American Convention Against Corruption, which calls on member states to criminalize bribery, and which is similar to the OECD Convention. The European Union in 1997 adopted a Convention on the Fight Against Corruption Involving Officials of the European Community or Officials of Member States of the European Union, which prohibits bribery of public officials within the European Union (EU), but does not prohibit the bribery of foreign nationals within the European Union or foreign officials from non-EU countries. In 1998, the Pacific Basin Economic Council, comprised of companies doing business in member countries of the Asia Pacific Economic Cooperation, adopted a Charter on Standards of Transactions between Business and Governments. This charter parallels the OECD convention and commands member companies to obey a code of corporate and ethical conduct. Finally, in Africa in 2006, the African Union adopted a Convention on Preventing and Combating Corruption, which requires member states to criminalize bribery and to protect whistleblowers. Weinograd (2010) noted a report in 2002 by the OECD's Working Group on Bribery and International Business Transactions, which criticized the FCPA's routine government action exception as "an area of risk," "open to misuse," and "unworkable" (p. 526).

China presents an interesting situation. Some writers are not certain that the Chinese government enforces anti-bribery laws against its business people bribing foreign government officials overseas. However, it is certain that the government enforces anti-bribery laws in China when it is a Chinese government official being bribed. The punishment, moreover, can be draconian. For example, the *Wall Street Journal* (Zamiska, Leow, and Oster, 2007), reported that a death sentence was imposed on the former head of a Chinese food and drug "watch-dog" government agency for receiving bribes of cash and gifts totaling at least $850,000 from eight pharmaceutical companies during his tenure at the State Food and Drug Administration. At the time, China was suffering from a series of food contaminations, and the country had announced the formation of a national food-recall system. The *Wall Street Journal* suggested that the harsh sentence was intended by the Chinese government to send a "stern message" about bribery, particularly regarding the safety of food and drugs; and the newspaper quoted a Chinese news source which stated that the death sentence was justified by the People's Court in Beijing due to the "huge amounts of bribes involved and the great damage inflicted on the country and the company by (the official's) dereliction of duty" (Zamiska, Leow, and Oster, 2007, A3). Zamiska, Leow, and Oster (2007) also noted that the Chinese news agency did not name the pharmaceutical companies who allegedly had bribed the government official.

Summary

This chapter examined important international anti-bribery and anti-corruption laws, with particular attention focused on the anti-bribery convention of the Organization for Economic Cooperation and Development. Other regional and national anti-bribery and anti-corruption laws were also briefly discussed. The next chapter will examine bribery in the context of culture and cultural conventions.

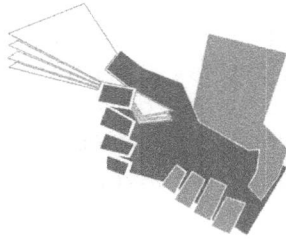

CHAPTER FOUR

Cultural Conventions and the Practice of Bribery

This chapter examines bribery in a cultural context and with reference to cultural conventions. The chapter discusses examples of bribery in various countries from around the world, featuring Afghanistan. It further provides data from Transparency International about Corruption Perception Index (CPI) in selected countries to see how they are ranked among the 180 countries in the study. Bribery is not just a Western or Eastern issue, but rather a universal concern that is impacting countries and human beings around the world.

Introduction and Overview

Bribery and other forms of corruption are intrinsically bound up with the social norms and practices of a society. Bribery is a common way of doing business in many societies; it is in many places an ingrained cultural practice. Actually, it can be, and often is, argued, that it is "culturally imperialistic" for the United States or other Western nations to impose their moral standards and "biases" on other perhaps less developed nations. The *Wall Street Journal* noted that at least up until the 1990s, some executives considered bribing foreign officials to be a "routine part of doing business" globally (Gold and Crawford, 2008, p. B1). Bribery usually is most prevalent in less developed countries, where jobs do not pay well, and thus it is considered to be customary for local government officials to "supplement" their income by taking such payments. In many countries, the payment of local and national government officials has been considered to be part of the "price of entry" to doing business in those countries. Kramer (2002) relates that:

> Officials typically demand bribes of 10 percent to 20 percent of the price to award a contract. This can amount to millions of dollars on a single contract....In some cases, bribes of 40 percent or more of project funds can be consumed as bribes....In countries with 'systemic' corruption the problem is well organized and entrenched with regular distribution channels persisting from regime to regime. The corruption affects every project and every contractor must pay. Project officials, supervising governmental officials, cabinet ministers, and sometimes the presidency, share the bribes proportionately (p. 24).

Of course, any proclivity to demand and to receive bribes is increased to the extent that government officials perceive themselves to be immune to any penalties that may exist under local law for demanding and receiving bribes (Allan, 2000). Spalding (2010) points out that the thrust of the FCPA is "to impact the supplier of bribes rather than the solicitors, recipients, or the governments that tolerate them" (p. 359). Spalding (2010) adds that "there is absolutely no part of the statute suggesting that the solicitor, recipient, or its government should be held responsible or punished for the bribe...The statute is thus 'supply-side' the 'demand-side' is well beyond its purview" (p. 366). Other factors further contributing to bribery and a "culture of corruption" in many countries are low salaries for government officials, weak criminal justice systems, and a perceived attitude of impunity to government sanctions due to long periods of entrenched one-party, one-faction, or one-person rule. Pelletier and Kottke (2009) note that "when discussing why people act in an unethical manner, one factor continues to emerge in the research; the person feels he or she can get away with it" (p. 83). Specifically regarding facilitating and expediting payments, Weinograd (2010) theorizes that their permissibility by the U.S. Congress represented a "realistic decision" since "members of the House and Senate recognized that in some countries grease payments are a common occurrence and may even be culturally permissible" (p. 534). Yet in some countries and cultures, bribery has gone way beyond "mere" grease; and bribery clearly can inhibit economic growth due to the deleterious effects of economic inefficiency and reduced investment which can occur on the national as well as corporate levels (Thomas, 2010).

To illustrate the extent and harmful effect of bribery, the *Wall Street Journal* (Walker, 2010) alleged in 2010 that a significant factor contributing to the financial and budget crisis adversely affecting Greece during the writing of this book is the level of corruption and bribery in that country. The newspaper stated that corruption is so engrained in that country that it is known for, and has its own names for, its two forms of corruption: bribery, called Fakelaki, meaning "little envelopes," and Rousfeti, meaning "expensive political favors. The *Wall Street Journal* asserted that "together, these traditions of corruption and cronyism have a produced a state that is both bloated and malnourished, and a crisis of confidence that is shaking all of Europe" (Walker, 2010, p. A1). The newspaper also reported a recent Brookings Institution study that found that "bribery, patronage, and other public corruption, are major contributors to the country's ballooning debt, depriving the Greek state each year of the equivalent of at least 8% of the gross domestic product or more than 20 billion Euros (about \$27 billion)" (Walker, 2010, pp. A1, A15). The reason for this level of corruption, which, according to the Greek Prime Minister, is "systemic," is the belief of the Greek people that "there is impunity in this country" (Walker, 2010, p. A15). The *Wall Street Journal* (Walker, 2010) also reported the findings of Transparency

International, the international anti-corruption organization, which did an international survey of countries' perceived graft. Greece came in last for corruption for the 27 member European Community, tied with Bulgaria and Romania. Transparency International also reported that in 2009, about 13.5% of Greek households paid a bribe, and that the average amount was 1,355 Euros. Also, as reported in the newspaper, the World Bank did a study which found that Greece came in last for the 16 member Euro zone countries for controlling corruption. Finally, and most disturbingly, the *Wall Street Journal* quoted a Greek professor who specializes in economic crime, who lamented that "the core of the problem is that we don't have a culture of civic society....In Greece, complying with the rules is a matter of dishonor. They call you stupid if you follow the rules" (Walker, 2010, p. A15).

In Nigeria, Timberg (2005) reported that "navigating the most basic government services, such as getting freight through customs, often requires a bribe....Motorists have little choice but to pay police officers – many armed with automatic rifles – who set up impromptu roadblocks to demand a 'kola nut.' The caffeine-laden nut is a traditional offering of hospitality in Nigeria, but to police the term refers to a wad of money worth anywhere from a few cents to several dollars" (p. 27A). However, for politicians in Nigeria, the bribery amounts naturally are much larger. The bribes are called "welfare payments" or "Ghana-Must-Go bags," which latter term refers to the colorful woven satchels used as suitcases in the 1980s when the Nigerian government was pressuring immigrants from nearby Ghana to return home. When filled, a Ghana-Must-Go bag can hold several hundred thousand dollars of currency (Timberg, 2005). For Mexico, the *Sun-Sentinel* (Dickerson, 2006) newspaper deemed bribery and corruption to be an "ongoing disaster" (p. 20A); and that Mexican government officials have estimated that as much as 9% of Mexico's gross domestic national product is siphoned off annually due to corruption (which would have amounted in 2005 to $69 billion). To illustrate, the *Sun-Sentinel* reported one situation where a restaurant owner in Mexico City was required to make an "under-the-table" payment of $1350 in order to secure a business operating license which the business owner was otherwise entitled to (Dickerson,

2006). The *Sun-Sentinel* (Dickerson, 2006) also reported that one out of every five businesses in Mexico admitted to making "extra-official" payments to government officials to obtain public contracts, speed up the processing of paperwork, circumvent regulations, or simply to have one's garbage picked up (which latter service requires payment of a weekly "tip").

India presents a picture very similar to Mexico, particularly concerning the payment of bribes to secure licenses and other approvals to open a business. National Public Radio (Kestenbaum, 2010) reported the saga of a young Indian entrepreneur, age 22, who wanted to start a business in his country delivering telephone and Internet service. He hired four people and was about to secure approval from the government for stringing up some wires as well as obtaining the necessary licenses. He soon realized that he was not going to get the necessary approvals without the payment of bribes. So, he related to National Public Radio that during an appointment with one government official, the young entrepreneur took out a folder filled with rupees (about $200) tucked inside, passed it to the government official who then slipped it into his briefcase. He was then offered tea and cookies by the official, who shortly thereafter gave his approval. The young entrepreneur further related that such payments were necessary almost every step during the process to secure the necessary government approvals, involving 10-15 government officials. Every official in the process from junior engineers to senior engineers to their managers had to be bribed. Then he had his cable lines established, but one building manager threatened to cut the cables unless he was paid, which, of course, he was, and now the building manager protects the cable lines. National Public Radio reported that the young entrepreneur thought of just leaving the county, but then was "educated" by his parents, who said that "every system in India works on this note," and that "you cannot run away." Most interestingly, the young entrepreneur related that his principles had changed; and as such now his "principles are to just get your things done. Everything is fair in love, war and business" (Kestenbaum, 2010). The reporter for National Public Radio also stated that he had spoken to many other people in India about bribery, from business owners to taxi drivers to ordinary people, and that many of them had a story about bribing someone in the government to get something done. Although people in India thought that bribery was unfair and a hassle, and they wished the practice would stop, nonetheless due to large government bureaucracy, all the paperwork, and the slowness of government agencies and the courts, it just made economic sense, they asserted, to bribe government officials. Yet when one does bribe a government official in India, one apparently gets "good service," as the bribed government official then becomes one's own personal *Ganesh*, who is the god known as the remover of obstacles (Kestenbaum, 2010).

Other examples of possible "grease" that were related to the authors of this book by their working, adult, graduate students include the following:

- The payment of $2500 to an official of a Caribbean country to get a company's telephone and utility services turned on and functioning.
- The attachment of a U.S. $100 bill to each application for the expeditious processing of firearms permits for private security personnel in a South American country.
- The payment of a U.S. $100 bill to facilitate each package of telecommunications equipment through customs in a Central American country.
- The payment of a U.S. $20 bill to the highway police in a Central American country to make sure that your vehicle paperwork and driver's license are proper.
- The transfer of several cases of expensive liquor to dock workers, supervisors, and port and customs officials to obtain the prompt and safe unloading and processing of large shipments of liquor to a South American country.
- The transfer to the wife of a military officer in a South American country of expensive bathroom and kitchen tile to facilitate the delivery of oil field equipment through a military checkpoint commanded by her husband.

Yet whether all these payments are sufficiently small and whether all the government officials involved are sufficiently lower level ones for the payments and transfers to be legal "grease" are good questions indeed!

Gift-giving, furthermore, in some cultures is an integral aspect of doing business. Yet a gift could be deemed an illegal bribe. To illustrate, Weinograd (2010) reported on gift-giving practices in South Korea, where the payments of Ttokkap, or "rice-cake expenses," are typical gifts given during the Korean Thanksgiving and on New Year's Day. To accommodate this established local cultural practice, as well as to avoid any legal implications, the Supreme Court of Korea has recognized a "social courtesy exception" to that country's anti-bribery laws. However, this gift must be offered as a mere social courtesy, and must not exceed "socially acceptable levels," which appears to be an ethically relativistic norm (Weinograd, 2010). Consequently, if payments are in excess of these usual and customary amounts, they may give rise to prosecution for bribery in South Korea as well as the opprobrium of the Korean people against businesses that attempt to manipulate their cherished cultural norms (Weinograd, 2010).

Transparency International, a private international anti-corruption and bribery organization, lists the most corrupt nations in the world based on perceptions of the prevalence of bribery (see Table 1). In 2000, the most corrupt nation was Cameroon followed by Nigeria and Indonesia; in 2002, the countries perceived to be the most corrupt in the world to be Bangladesh, Nigeria, and Uganda, and the least corrupt countries were Finland, Denmark, and New Zealand; in 2005, the most corrupt nation was Bangladesh followed by Haiti and Nigeria; and in 2009, the most corrupt was Somalia followed by Afghanistan and Myanmar. Complete year-to-year listings on global corruption can be found at the Transparency International website (www.globalcorruptionreport.org). In 2006, the *Economist* (October 14, 2006) reported that India, China, and Russia were the "most prolific bribe-payers while doing business abroad," while Switzerland, Sweden, and Australia were the least likely to bribe (p. 106). The U.S. was ranked tenth out of 30 countries as to frequency of bribes paid with the top category being "bribes never paid" and the bottom category being "bribes are common" (Economist, October 14, 2006, p. 106). See Table 1 for the 2009 data from Transparency International, where the United States is ranked 19 on the Corruption Perception Index.

The prevalence of bribery as reported by Transparency International should decrease due to international anti-corruption efforts. Spalding (2010) relates that regarding the OECD anti-bribery convention, "the adoption of that convention marked a sea change in worldwide attitudes toward bribery and the emergence of an international, but not universal, commitment to the principle to enforcing bribery prohibitions" (pp. 353-54).

Table 1 – Corruption Perception Index
(Transparency International, 2009)

Rank	Country/Territory for 2009 Scores	CPI	Rank	Country/Territory for 2009 Scores	CPI
1	New Zealand	9.4	89	Mexico	3.3
2	Denmark	9.3	99	Domin. Republic	3.0
3	Singapore	9.2	99	Jamaica	3.0
3	Sweden	9.2	106	Argentina	2.9
5	Switzerland	9.0	111	Egypt	2.8
6	Finland	8.9	111	Indonesia	2.8
6	Netherlands	8.9	120	Kazakistan	2.7
8	Australia	8.7	120	Vietnam	2.7
8	Canada	8.7	130	Lebanon	2.5
8	Iceland	8.7	130	Libya	2.5
11	Norway	8.6	130	Nigeria	2.5
12	Hong Kong	8.2	130	Uganda	2.5
17	Japan	7.7	139	Bangladesh	2.4
17	UK	7.7	139	Pakistan	2.4
19	United States	7.5	139	Philippines	2.4
24	France	6.9	143	Azerbaijan	2.3
30	UAE	6.5	146	Russia	2.2
32	Spain	6.1	154	Yemen	2.1
37	Taiwan	5.6	158	Cambodia	2.0
39	Oman	5.5	158	Laos	2.0
49	Jordan	5.0	158	Tajikistan	2.0
49	Poland	5.0	162	Kyrgyzstan	1.9
55	South Africa	4.7	162	Venezuela	1.9
56	Malaysia	4.5	168	Haiti	1.8
61	Cuba	4.4	168	Iran	1.8
61	Turkey	4.4	168	Turkmenistan	1.8
63	Italy	4.3	174	Uzbekistan	1.7
63	Saudi Arabia	4.3	176	Iraq	1.5
71	Greece	3.8	178	Myanmar	1.4
75	Brazil	3.7	179	Afghanistan	1.3
75	Colombia	3.7	180	Somalia	1.1
79	China	3.6			
79	Trinidad & Tobago	3.6			
84	India	3.4			
84	Thailand	3.4			

Source: Transparency International, 2009. Retrieved on April 20, 2010 from: http://transparency.org/policy_research/surveys_indices/cpi/2009

Culture and Bribery

Culture is made up of the way people think, decide, feel, act, and respond to things in a given location; and is based on such common characteristics as location, climate, language, religion, and other such factors. As Geert Hofsteded (1980) defined the concept, culture is the collective programming of people's mind (which involves thinking, feeling, and acting), that distinguishes them from other human beings. People of different cultures have different norms, customs, and mores based on their years of socialization in a society. For example, during or before a wedding in Afghanistan, the groom's family is expected to provide a sum of money (as determined by the bride's family) to the bride's parents for raising her, providing her education and training, taking care of the wedding expenses, and for the bride to take care of herself and future children in the case of divorce or the groom's death. Such customs are often reversed in other societies where the bride's family takes care of the wedding expenses.

When it comes to corruption and bribery, some people claim that there is a "cultural convergence" in today's individualistic and self-centered world. Cultural convergence is a view that people around the globe are increasingly seeing the same news, hearing the same concepts, learning the same knowledge, desiring the same outcomes, and, as a result, are thinking and acting alike. This cultural convergence can be illustrated from the increasingly widespread use and acceptance of bribes. Bribes, which are payments in cash or kind in order to unduly influence officials to grant business "favors," are likely to be found in every culture. As presented previously, bribery can be seen as one form of corruption, along with other inducements, enticements, buying-off, kickbacks, embezzlement, subornment, paying-off, and other corruptions to the system. Some of the common terms for bribery across different countries and cultures are presented in Table 2.

The word *"baksheesh,"* which is derived from the Persian[2] (Dari) word commonly pronounced as "bakhshish" in Afghanistan, is one that conveys feelings of appreciation by providing a tip, for example, to a waiter, or a reward for a job well done. For example, if a person loses his or her wallet, and another person finds it, then the finder might be given an amount of say $100 as *bakhshish* or reward. Another pertinent word in Persian (Dari) speaking countries, such as Afghanistan and Iran, is *Roshwat*, meaning bribe. The term *Roshwat Khoordan* implies taking a bribe (the word *"Khoordan"* literally means eating); and the term *Roshwat Khoory* means bribery. Finally, the term *Roshwat Khoor* describes the person who is taking a bribe.

Table 2 – Equivalent Words for Bribery in Different Cultures

Locations	Term for Bribery
Afghanistan, Iran, Pakistan	Roshwat
Africa	Dash
Southeast Asia	Kumshaw
Brazil	Jeitinho
France	Pot au vin
Germany	Trink Gelt / Schmiergeld
Greece	Baksissi
Hong Kong	Hatchien
India, Iran, Afghanistan, Turkey, and Egypt	Baksheesh (Bakhsheesh)
Italy	Bustarella
Japan	Wairo
Malaysia	Makan Siap
Mexico	La mordida
Philippines	Lagay
Russia	Vzyatha
Thailand	Sin bone
United States	Grease money (greasing the wheels), payola

---

[2] *Presentation at the Society of Afghan Engineers (SAE/SAAE) Conference.* July 12-15, 2010. Kabul Polytechnic University, Afghanistan.

Regardless of the term used, the unfortunate side of bribery is that it hurts people, cities, countries, and societies overall. While some governments have specific rules and enforceable policies in place to combat bribery, others allow some forms of payments to government officials, or do not enforce their stated local laws and treaties prohibiting bribery. For example, McFarlin and Sweeney (2006, p. 87) state that "In France, paying off foreigners can be written off as a tax deduction." There have been many examples of firms and individuals across different continents and countries that have been accused of taking bribes or bribing others; and the following are some noteworthy examples or accusations of wrongdoing (McFarlin and Sweeney, 2006, pp. 87-102):

- In 1995, Lockheed Martin paid $24 million in fines and its executive was imprisoned for bribing Egyptian government officials in the amount of $1.5 million to secure an aircraft contract / deal.
- General Electric (GE) paid a fine of $69 million when it was discovered that one of their employees bribed an Israeli general.
- Officials in France were said to have offered aid to Vietnam in order to secure part of the Vietnamese telecom market.
- Officials in France supposedly said that they would pull loan guarantees to an African country unless the French firm was given the $20 million telecom contract.
- A European aerospace company said it would lobby against Turkey joining the European Union unless Turkey purchased its airplanes.
- High-tech firms in Germany bribed officials to win eleven contracts over a ten-year period.
- Japanese officials had offered to cancel Brazil's $30 million debt to Tokyo if they purchased a supercomputer from a firm in Japan which cost about the same amount.
- High-ranking Indian government officials were indicted on corruption and extortion charges—some of these involved American firms, including the former Enron Corporation.

- A bad loan scandal in the amount of $350 billion in Japan exposed unethical cooperation between political leaders, bankers, and criminal gangs.
- Chairman of South Korea's SK Corp only served three months in prison for a multi-billion dollar tax fraud.
- The Chinese government investigated over 43,000 cases of graft and corruption in 2001.
- Political leaders in Moscow have threatened investigations and legislation changes to stop big corporations from receiving unfair assistance from their "uncles" (dyadyas) working in the public sector.
- A former consultant to the Afghan Ministry of Mines and Industry reported that a Minister in Afghanistan was supposedly paid a $20 million bribe by Chinese contractors to award the development of Aynak project for copper mining to their state-owned China Metallurgical Group (MMC) firm.

As presented by Transparency International, which is a Berlin, Germany-based private organization devoted to stamping out corrupt business practices, the Corruption Perceptions Index (CPI) is designed to measure the perceived level of corruption in the public-sector. Transparency International's CPI is a "survey of surveys," based on business surveys conducted by at least thirteen different experts. The Corruption Perceptions Index (CPI) data shows a country's ranking and score for data compiled in 2009. In the Transparency International study, an index score of 10.0 means no corruption, whereas a CPI score of 0.0 means the country is likely to be highly corrupt. In this case, the CPI score for each country indicates the "perceived level of public-sector corruption" as determined by Transparency International findings.

Corruption is not necessarily a characteristic of poverty as it can exist in any society and environment. Yet, data shows that the least corrupt countries in 2009 were New Zealand, Denmark, Singapore, Sweden, Switzerland, Finland, Netherlands, Australia, Canada, Iceland, Norway, and Hong Kong. As such, from a fairness and rule of law perspective, these are considered to be excellent places for investment, entrepreneurship, and international business. On the other extreme, the most corrupt places in 2009 by International Transparency study were Cambodia, Laos, Tajikistan, Kyrgyzstan, Venezuela, Haiti, Iran, Turkmenistan, Uzbekistan, Iraq, Sudan, Myanmar, Afghanistan, and Somalia. Of course, a country's citizens as well as political and business leaders should attempt to report cases of bribery and not tolerate corruption in order to have a culture and country where people from around the world would want to come for pleasure, business, and investment opportunities.

Bribery and Corruption in Afghanistan

Bribery, corruption, and other such secretly conducted deleterious practices can sooner or later lead to unfortunate outcomes and bring misery – economical, political, social, and even militarily. Afghanistan is such a case. In one very unfortunate incident, ten French soldiers died because they had incorrectly assessed the danger in Afghanistan. During August and September of 2009, it was widely reported that the French personnel in Afghanistan asserted that the Italian Secret Service had been secretly paying certain "local warlords" in exchange for the safety and protection of the Italian Army in the Uzbin Valley at the Surobi District of Afghanistan. Yet when the French soldiers took over that territory in July of that year they said they were never told about the bribes, and consequently made a "catastrophically incorrect threat assessment." The French officials thus blamed the loss of ten of their soldiers in one ambush on August 18, 2009 in the Uzbin Valley on the Italian Secret Service. Previously, the Italians that were in the area experienced no serious violence; the Italians only had lost one soldier in the previous one year. The French officials claimed that since the French Army knew nothing of the bribery payments, the army made a catastrophically inaccurate assessment of the threat in the village, resulting in the deaths of their soldiers.

In another equally disturbing bribery story involving the military in Afghanistan, the *Sun-Sentinel* newspaper (Rodriquez,

2010) reported that some business people in Pakistan and Afghanistan are paying bribes to police, politicians, and government bureaucrats to allow the transport of caravans of trucks carrying ammonium nitrate fertilizer. The substance is used by the insurgents to make bombs, particularly roadside bombs, that have killed so many soldiers – U.S., Western, and Afghan – as well as civilians. The substance was used by Afghan farmers as a fertilizer, but the U.S. government pressured the Afghan government to ban it in the country. However, the substance is legal in Pakistan, but there are many military and police checkpoints along the Pakistan-Afghanistan highway; and consequently there are many public officials to bribe to get the caravans through to their Afghan destinations. A caravan typically has at least 12 trucks; each truck can carry 130 bags containing about 110 pounds each of the substance; the caravan thus can move about 85 tons of the substance, and in one night. Eighty five tons of ammonium nitrate fertilizer can make about 2500 bombs. Once the substance is smuggled into Afghanistan by the Pakistani trucking companies, Afghan middlemen then sell and distribute it to the insurgents, who use it to make bombs. The *Sun-Sentinel* (Rodriquez, 2010) quoted one of the businessmen involved in the smuggling, who said that they all know the substance is used to make bombs to kill local and foreign soldiers, but the people involved have no choice as there is no other way to make money, and the tribal areas of Afghanistan are very poor. The businessman was not named in the newspaper article.

Many military and political analysts have reflected on how widespread such pay-off practices might be in Afghanistan. The answer seems very clear; such practices are very widespread. In fact, private contractors and government officials often pay bribes to get their supplies and convoys through dangerous areas in Afghanistan. Yet ultimately, business leaders, government officials, and political leaders should not tolerate illegal and unethical practices, as this cycle of corruption will hurt the country and its economy and people.

Today, many claim that drugs and bribery make up the two largest income generating avenues in Afghanistan. As such, the country is very much open to being taken advantage of by thugs, thieves, gangsters, corrupt officials, and greedy contractors and multinationals, as they all apparently can do whatever they want to maximize profits and enrich themselves in one of the poorest countries in the world. According to Gebauer and Volkery (2010), if one needs a driver's license in Kabul of Afghanistan, securing it is not a problem as one can obtain it for "only" a payment $180 and expeditiously too within hours. Furthermore, an amount of about $60,000 can get a drug smuggler out of jail within a few weeks to no longer than a few months. Afghanistan, therefore, is seeing rampant corruption; and the amount of money being exchanged in bribery is about equal to a quarter of the Afghan GDP (Gebauer and Volkery, 2010). Most people know exactly how big the bribery and corruption problem is in Afghanistan as everything is possible for a price. In such a corrupt environment, the rich tend to get richer and the poor will "at best" remain in status quo despite their diligent efforts and hard work to improve their station in life. Many business people, contractors, visitors, and expatriates in Kabul claim nothing is accomplished during a given day in Afghanistan without someone receiving the payment of a bribe.

According to the 2010 report by the United Nations Office on Drugs and Crime (UNODC, 2010), based on the responses of 7,600 people from 1,600 Afghan villages, about 59% of Afghans see corruption as the greatest problem for the country. Corruption and bribery practices (59%) are often seen as a greater problem than security (54%) and unemployment (52%). Afghan citizens have supposedly paid about $2.5 billion in bribes. The study reported that 39% of women and 53% of men had actually paid a bribe to a government official during the past one year. In about 40 percent of the contracts and paperwork needing signatures in government offices cases, citizens were asked for bribes in order to get their work done in a timely manner. Actually, over 50% of those surveyed reported having bribed someone within the past 12 months; and the payments average around $158, which can be a huge burden for a teacher as it is equivalent to one to two months of his/her salary. In Afghanistan, the average annual income is about $42; therefore, many people cannot even afford to bribe officials. The *Miami Herald* (Rodriguez, 2010) reported in 2010 that Afghanistan is now so plagued by "endemic corruption," according to a United Nations report, that the level of corruption amounts to a "virtual tax" on the people, "robbing them" of about one quarter of the nation's annual gross domestic product (p. 15A). Concerning bribery, the average amount of a bribe in Afghanistan is approximately "only" $160 (which obviously is a great deal of money for the poverty-stricken Afghans), but what was startling in the U.N. report was the fact that one out of every two Afghan people reported at least making one payment to a public official within a year. The *Miami Herald* reported that for 2009 Afghans paid about $2.5 billion in bribes; and furthermore the Afghans related that they were asked to pay bribes in 40% of their dealings with senior government officials (Rodriquez, 2010).

The widespread presence of bribery and corruption among government officials, police officers, and judicial members is very dangerous, as these harmful practices will keep the cycle of poverty and misery spiraling further downward. In the more rural part of the country, corruption and bribery are at their highest levels. Many foreigners claim that these high levels of bribery and corrupt practices are part of a long tradition of patronage and nepotism in Afghanistan; thus, some level of corruption is considered to be socially acceptable, proper, and legitimate, as certain practices are "merely" considered a "present," "bakhsheesh," or even "Shookrana" (that is, a token of "thank you"). These "presents" are mainly are in the form of cash, but at times in the forms of livestock, part of the harvest, clothes, cloth, food, and other such valuable commodities in the local villages.

There are billions of dollars from the international community being spent in Afghanistan by different organizations and agencies, each advancing its own agenda, but without much integration toward a "holistic" view of what is good for the entire country and its people. Politicians at low levels seem to have acquired money, prestige, and power due to corruption and bribery practices. There is the official government; and then there is the "shadow government" involved in corrupt practices, such as charging $25,000 to settle lawsuits, $6,000 to bribe the police for getting out of blatant legal violations that can result in imprisonment, and $100,000 to secure a job as a provincial police chief, which then can lead to taking enormous amounts of bribes and kickbacks while in office. It is obvious that most governments in developing economies are likely to experience similar forms of corruption. However, the level of corruption in Afghanistan is unprecedented since the country has gone from a Transparency International ranking 117 out of 180 countries in 2005 to 179 in 2009. Afghan government officials, therefore, must spend much of their time and resources to combat all this bribery and corruption, while devising and implementing a suitable public affairs strategy to reduce the negative perceptions of the country caused by such bribery and corruption.

Yet the situation in Afghanistan regarding the prevalence and toleration of corruption and bribery may be changing, and perhaps changing in a way that puts that country and its government in a positive light. To illustrate, Rosenberg and Zahori (2010) in the *Wall Street Journal* reported that an Afghanistan court sentenced a British national to two years in prison for bribing two Afghan government officials. The conviction was noteworthy, declared the *Wall Street Journal*, because it was the first conviction of a foreigner on bribery and corruption charges in Afghanistan. The decision by the court is being hailed in Afghanistan as a major victory in that country's fight against corruption. However, Rosenberg and Zahori (2010) also reported that some, perhaps cynical, Western officials stated that the conviction looked like more of an effort by the Afghan government to "make an example" out of a foreigner while doing little to combat corruption at high levels in the Afghan government. Nevertheless, other Western officials stated that they were hopeful that the bribery conviction, even of a foreigner, would give the Afghan government the "political cover" it needed to commence prosecuting Afghan government officials (Rosenberg and Zahori, 2010). In the bribery conviction, the British national, age 56, was the manager at a British security firm. He was convicted of paying a $25,000 bribe to two government officials to obtain the release of a pair of Toyota Land Cruisers that had been seized by the police because they lacked proper registration. In addition to the prison sentence, the British manager had to pay a $25,000 fine. He did admit to paying the two officials, who were members of Afghanistan's Directorate of Security, but he maintained that he thought he was paying a legal and proper fine for the lack of the registrations, and he stated that he had asked for a receipt which he had not received as of the time of his arrest. He is now appealing his conviction. The *Wall Street Journal* pointed out that the conviction was imposed by a special anti-corruption tribunal, which had been established by the Afghan President, who has been "under intense pressure from the United States and other Western countries to take stronger action against corrupt officials" (Rosenberg and Zahori, 2010, p. A11). So far, the newspaper reported that a few Afghan government officials have been convicted by the tribunal, but most were low and middle level officials.

Summary

Bribery is a global concern, and business and government leaders from around the world must do what they can to eliminate this form of corruption. This chapter examined bribery in diverse cultural contexts and provided examples from different countries, featuring Afghanistan. This chapter further provided data from Transparency International about Corruption Perception Index (CPI) in various countries to emphasize how widespread the challenge of corruption can be for expatriates and business and government global leaders. The next chapter discusses bribery and ethics, while discussing various theories for effective and moral decision-making purposes.

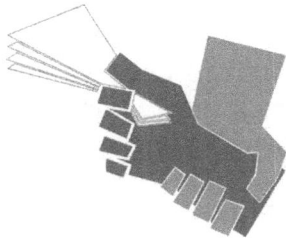

CHAPTER FIVE

Ethics and the Morality of Bribery

This chapter examines bribery from the perspectives of philosophical ethics and applied ethics in order to ascertain the morality of making bribes. Certain major ethical theories are used to determine the morality of bribery, with particular emphasis on the culturally based ethical theory of Ethical Relativism.

Introduction

Even if a bribe is legal, the question very well may emerge as to whether it is moral to pay a bribe. Moral issues bring one into the field of ethics, which is, of course, a branch of philosophy. It is first important to note the critical distinction between morality and ethics, to wit: morality is the conclusion as to what is good or bad or right or wrong. How that conclusion is ascertained is determined ethically, that is, by reference to ethical theories and principles and their application to a situation to reason to a moral conclusion. Ethics, therefore, is the intellectual framework that one applies to make moral conclusions or to create moral rules and precepts. Yet, there is one big problem with the field of ethics; and that is there are many ethical theories; and at times they are directly in conflict; and, moreover, there is no "Supreme Court of Ethics" to inform people what is the "true" ethical theory. Consequently, where one "lands" morally often depends on where one "stands" ethically.

Applied Ethics and the Morality of Bribery

In order to explicate major ethical theories and the moral aspects of bribery in an international setting, assume a situation where a sales and marketing representative of a U.S. multinational in precarious financial condition is in the final stages of negotiating a contract for the sale of a substantial quantity of goods to the government of a rapidly developing foreign country. The contract is very important to the company because it provides a significant infusion of money as well as an entry to a foreign market. The contract, moreover, personally is very important to the company's marketing/sales representative and would secure the representative a promotion and substantial raise. All appears to be proceeding well. The company's offer is viewed very favorably by the foreign government and the foreign country would in fact secure a very good deal by accepting the U.S. multinational's offer to contract. The U.S. multinational's representative seems assured of success until the representative is confronted by a key foreign government official, who also looks upon the company's offer favorably but demands a large "consulting fee" to properly process the paperwork and thus secure the contract. If the fee is not paid, the official will reopen the bidding and the contract may go to a competitor. The company's representative is acutely aware of the critical nature of the deal, knows that the sum is immaterial when compared to the contract price and the profits to be realized; and also has heard that such payments are a common and not unlawful practice in the foreign country; but feels that making such payments are not quite right and may be illegal under U.S. law. What is the "right", moral decision for the representative to make? Such an inquiry leads one directly into the field of applied ethics.

If one is a Legal Positivist, one would equate legality with morality; and thus one simply would advise the representative to determine the legality of the payment. If it is legal under the foreign country's law, and it is legal under the Foreign Corrupt Practices Act exception for expediting and facilitating payments for ministerial actions (such as, perhaps, the mere processing of the lowest bid), or due to its express legality pursuant to the host country's laws, then this legal action is also a moral action pursuant to Legal Positivism.

If one is an Ethical Emotist, one would base one's moral conclusion on one's emotional reaction and feelings of approval or disapproval; and accordingly the Ethical Emotist would advise the representative to get in "touch" with his or her feelings. If he or she feels "bad" about the payment, then it is immoral; if "good," then it is moral. Of course, he or she can always have a "change of heart" by merely having a different emotion about the payment at a later, perhaps more critical, date.

If one adheres to the doctrine of Ethical Egoism, the analysis is twofold: is it in the representative's best long-term interest, as agent of the multinational, to pay the bribe; and is it in the interest of the multinational, as the corporate entity, for its representative to pay the bribe? The representative must calculate whether the risks to his or her career, reputation, conscience, and even freedom will supersede the potential personal benefits from paying the bribe, securing the contract, and thus the promotion and raise. The multinational must determine whether the assertion and defense of its legitimate and critical business interests in the foreign country are worth the legal risks as well as risks to the company's reputation. An intelligent Ethical Egoist also could argue that even if the "bribe" is deemed immoral, the fact that its nonpayment is such a dangerous threat to the company's very existence, the issue of duress as a moral defense arises to counter any charge of immorality.

An Ethical Relativist bases his or her moral determinations on what a particular society believes is moral or immoral; and consequently the Ethical Relativist simply would tell the company and its representative to ascertain whether such payments are an accepted standard and locally unobjectionable practice in the foreign country; if so, paying the "bribe" may be quite moral. Ethical Relativism is a very important ethical theory for the international business person; and accordingly will be covered further and illustrated in the next major section of this chapter.

A Utilitarian, of course, would be concerned with the consequences of paying or not paying the bribe. Pursuant to Utilitarianism, an action is good and moral if it produces the greatest amount of good for the greatest number of people; and conversely it is immoral if it produces more bad consequences than good ones. Accordingly, if the bribe is not paid, the company, its shareholders, employees, and suppliers all will suffer a severe financial loss. If, however, the bribe is paid, all these preceding groups benefit, as well as the sales representative, who gets a promotion and raise; the foreign official, who gets the money; the foreign government, which gets a "good" price for a "good" product; and the foreign consumers, who get a quality product. If the bribe is paid, the competition does not get the contract; yet none of the company's competitors had the low bid anyway, so what is the real harm? Paying a bribe, however, usually is construed as adversely affecting the society of the "host" country. Bribery's net effect is to reduce market competition by engendering unequal competition and by erecting additional barriers to market entry. The "best" bribers thus begin to achieve monopoly status, with the distinct possibility of exhibiting the inefficiencies characteristic of monopolies, such as higher prices and lower quality. However, if this instance of bribery under consideration is viewed as an exception, and if one is an Act Utilitarian, which subjects narrowly stated actions to the Utilitarian test, the harm to society is reduced accordingly, and thus this "pain" is subject to being outweighed by the greater good produced for all the other affected groups and people.

Disregard these consequences - good or otherwise - of paying the bribe, a Kantian would argue. Rather, apply the Categorical Imperative – Kant's supreme ethical principle - to determine if bribery is moral. Pursuant to the Categorical Imperative, an action is moral if it can be made consistently universal, treats all people with dignity and respect, and would be acceptable to a rational person if this person did not know whether he or she would be the "agent," that is, the giver, or the receiver of the action. Applying the first test, a Kantian would argue that bribery cannot be realized as a consistently universal practice. Assuming everyone bribed in a similar fashion, the action "bribe" would no longer be able to sustain itself. Since everyone is bribing, "bribing" loses its efficacy; it contradicts itself, becomes nonsensical, and self-destructs. Bribery, therefore, is immoral.

Bribery with qualification, however, is a different matter. Bribery, in the case herein, saves one's company from financial ruin, secures a contract that is a "good deal" for the host government and country when the bribing company is in fact the lowest bidder, and induces the foreign government official to perform his or her public duty of merely awarding the contract. With such qualifications, "bribery" can be made consistently universal. Not everyone is bribing, and the bribe, because it is qualified, will secure results in the limited circumstances presented.

Although bribery qualified arguably can pass Kant's first test, the issue arises as to whether a qualified bribery action will pass the second and third parts of the Categorical Imperative. Does bribery treat all the parties involved with dignity and respect, particularly the official and the company's representative "pressured" to pay the bribe? Would paying the bribe be acceptable to a rational person if he or she did not know his or her status as the "giver" (or agent) of the action or the receiver? Would a rational person want to be placed in the role of the competition in a bribery scenario? Such questions clearly illustrate the strictness of Kantian ethics and the difficulty of even a qualified "wrongful" action passing the Categorical Imperative. Yet, a Kantian moral conclusion will only suffice if one is a Kantian! As emphasized, there are several ethical theories, and the selection of one particular theory to apply to the payment of a bribe very well could result in a differing moral conclusion.

Ethical v. Cultural Relativism and the Morality of Bribery

As emphasized, Ethical Relativism is a major ethical theory, and one that has significant ramifications for the international business person. In the United States, bribery is illegal and frowned upon by society as immoral. In some other countries, however, there is a culture of doing business through what many in the U.S. would deem illegal and immoral, that is, bribery. This "foreign" culture may even extend bribery to government officials under the rationale that such payments are "just what our culture expects." Reporting cultural beliefs and practices and pointing out differences among cultures are integral aspects of Cultural Relativism, which is merely a descriptive doctrine. Cultural Relativism simply says that there are different countries, societies, and cultures which may have distinct yet different mores and standards. Cultural Relativism just reports these differences; there is no moral component to this doctrine. However, there is clearly a moral component to the ethical theory of Ethical Relativism, which is not only a descriptive doctrine, but a prescriptive one too. That is, Ethical Relativism sets up these cultural differences and practices as moral norms. Ethical Relativism is a very ancient and established ethical theory in Western Civilization, going back to ancient Greece in the Fifth Century B.C. with the thoughts of the Sophists and their philosophical "school" founded on relativism. The Sophists denied that there were any universal, objective, moral truths; morality, as well as justice and religion, were totally and "merely" relative. From these cardinal principles evolved the doctrine of Ethical Relativism. If one is an Ethical Relativist, morality is determined by what a particular society believes is moral. That is, what a particular society believes is moral, is in fact moral, for that society. Consequently, if one is an Ethical Relativist, one "merely" has to adopt the practices and adhere to the mores of the host company, presuming they are considered to be morally acceptable in that society, and consequently one will be acting in a moral manner. If one is an Ethical Relativist, one will abjure from imposing any perceived universal values across and among societies since each society has its own unique, and true for itself, values system and moral beliefs and standards, including those relating to corruption and bribery. One does not need a doctoral degree in philosophy to be an Ethical Relativist; rather one just needs "sharp eyes and ears" to find out what goes on "on the ground." Get "educated" in the very practical sense to the term as to the accepted practices in a society; and then "When in Rome, do as the Romans," knowing that by so doing one will be acting not only in a culturally competent manner but also, significantly, a moral manner too!

So, if it is considered morally appropriate in the host county to make certain payments to foreign officials then it is, if one is an Ethical Relativist, also moral to do so, based on at least that ethical theory. How can one condemn bribery as wrong, if it is an accepted and standard practice in the host county if one is an Ethical Relativist. Of course, problems will ensue if such culturally and morally accepted practices, such as bribery, are also illegal pursuant to the law of the home country such as in the case of the FCPA, or considered to be immoral by virtue of another ethical theory, such as Utilitarianism, Kantian ethics or Aristotle's Virtue Ethics. In such cases, if business in the host country cannot be conducted in an effective manner without adopting the illegal or immoral local common practice, the company must be prepared to withdraw from the host country and forego the business opportunities. Despite the existence of Ethical Relativism as an established ethical theory in Western philosophy, commentators warn of the perils of an ethically relativistic point of view in the context of international business: "The U.S. government requires businesses and individuals to act ethically as they develop opportunities in foreign countries. The axiom "When in Rome, do as the Romans" is not only obsolete, but potentially devastating to business" (Bishop and Johnson, 2009, p. 25). Dworsky (2009) reflects that as more international efforts to eliminate corruption and bribery in international business are adopted, a major change in traditional societal views of corruption and bribery may be forthcoming. If that is the case, then Ethical Relativism, which has been popularly called the "best friend" ethically of the global business person, may become his or her "worst enemy."

Summary

This chapter examined bribery from the perspectives of philosophical ethics and applied ethics in order to ascertain the morality of making bribes. Certain major ethical theories were used to determine the morality of bribery, with particular emphasis being placed on the culturally based ethical theory of Ethical Relativism. The next chapter will present an actual bribery case.

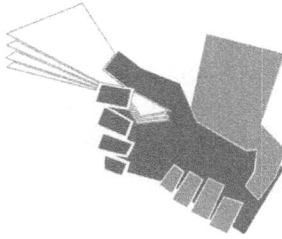

CHAPTER SIX

The Salt Lake City Olympic Bribery Case

This chapter presents and discusses an actual bribery prosecution and court case based on the Foreign Corrupt Practices Act. The authors review the famous (infamous?) case of the Salt Lake City Olympic bribery scandal, which will serve to illustrate several legal, ethical, and practical issues relating to bribery and the FCPA. The chapter also provides discussion questions at the end of the case which can be used for analytical, discussion, and training purposes.

Case Facts and Legal History

In December 1998, the U.S. Justice Department announced that it was reviewing allegations that Olympic organizers in Salt Lake City might have engaged in bribery of International Olympic Committee (IOC) members as part of a successful effort to bring the 2002 games to Utah. Attorney General Janet Reno at the time acknowledged that Justice's Criminal Division had launched an inquiry after the Salt Lake Organizing Committee (SLOC) admitted paying tuition, expenses, and fees for several relatives of IOC members. Investigators at Justice attempted to determine whether the SLOC violated the Foreign Corrupt Practices Act, which prohibits the bribery of foreign officials, in this case the IOC officials. In addition, tax fraud was part of the investigation since the Justice Department investigators sought to determine whether tax exempt money had been misused by buying gifts or funding scholarships for relatives of members of the IOC.

The issue of vote buying arose because of the disclosure of scholarship payments made to six relatives of IOC members by Salt Lake City officials during their successful bid to play host to the 2002 winter games. The SLOC has said the payments, which amounted to slightly less than $400,000, came from a privately financed fund that was started in 1991. Moreover, the Justice Department investigated Intermountain Health Care, Utah's largest health care provider, which confirmed that it gave free surgical services worth $28,000 to at least two people associated with the IOC. The surgery included knee replacement surgery for an IOC member, and plastic surgery to smooth the bags under the eyes of one person associated with the IOC. The price to stage the 2002 Winter Games was at the time already up to $1.4 billion; and the SLOC's bid process cost $13 million. Tax forms filed by the SLOC did not include entries for the scholarship program. Cash payments ranging from $5,000 up to $70,000 to IOC members from Africa and Latin America also were investigated, as well as a Utah land deal, arranged by Committee officials that turned a quick $60,000 profit for IOC member Jean-Claude Ganga of the Republic of Congo. Expensive gifts, including a pair of shotguns, worth $2,000, for IOC President, Juan Antonio Samaranch, were also reportedly given. Finally, a Salt Lake ethics panel looked into possible use of Committee credit cards to pay for "female escorts" for IOC members. IOC rules forbid members from accepting anything worth more than $150 from bidders. In another case, a delegate from Libya was flown in from Tripoli to visit Salt Lake City and to view the Olympic sites, but a good portion of the delegate's trip was spent not in Salt Lake City, but rather in Paris, which was one of the interconnecting air cities.

Marc Holder, an 80 year old lawyer, a Swiss IOC member, member of the IOC's Executive Board, and former head of the International Ski Federation, stated that he believed that several IOC members and their agents had been involved in vote buying the past 10 years; and he said he thought 5 to 7 percent of IOC members, at the time numbering 115, were open to bribery. He also said that there was one agent of an IOC member who boasts that "no city has ever won the Olympic Games without his help." Agents promise, according to Holder, to deliver blocs of IOC votes. Frank Joklik, president of the SLOC, apologized and accepted full responsibility for the scholarship program run by the group that won the bid for the games. The program provided the $400,000 in tuition and other assistance to 13 individuals, including six relatives of IOC members, mostly from Africa. Only one recipient of the scholarship fund had been identified, the daughter of an IOC member from Cameroon, Africa. It was also reported that the son of a Libyan IOC member listed the Salt Lake bid committee's address on his application to Brigham Young University.

Holder had used the word "bribe" to describe the scholarship fund. "With hindsight, I believe this program should not have been part of the bid campaign," Joklik said. Yet, he said he still supported giving academic aid and athletic training to youngsters from developing countries, professing the "humanitarian" and "educational" purposes thereto; but acknowledged that "it should not be done in a way that might possibly appear to influence improperly the voting of IOC members." Nonetheless, Joklik steadfastly maintained that it was not the SLOC's intent to bribe IOC members. In January of 1999, Jolik and Dave Johnson, the committee's senior vice-president, resigned under pressure. Both denied personal knowledge of these activities. Holder, moreover, raised the scandal to global proportions when he claimed irregularities in the election campaigns awarding the Summer Games to Atlanta in 1996 and Sydney in 2000 and the Winter Games to Nagano in 1998. He charged that the Olympic selection process is riddled with corruption, with agents demanding up to $1 million to deliver votes. Officials in Beijing, moreover, accused Sydney of buying the 2000 vote.

According to interviews and news accounts at the time, Salt Lake City decided it would concentrate its courting of delegates from Africa and Latin America. The feeling was that finalists, Ostersund, Sweden, and Sion, Switzerland, likely had the support of most European IOC members, and that Quebec's bid might neutralize Salt Lake City's support in North America. A Quebec City newspaper quoted a 2002 bid official who said at least three agents claiming IOC ties offered to swing the vote away from Salt Lake City, which eventually won by a 54-14 vote margin. Ironically, Salt Lake City did not need the African votes; and because the balloting is secret, SLOC could not even be sure it had gotten the votes it is accused of paying for.

The scandal tarnished the reputations of Salt Lake City and Utah, ignited opposition to letting the city play host to the Games, and had provoked "second thoughts" by at least one major corporate sponsor. The allegations jeopardized a $50 million pledge of sponsorship from US West Inc., a telecommunications company, which withhold its first payment of $5 million, until it gained more information on the scandal. Local organizers and the U.S. Olympic Committee feared that it would be difficult to raise the remaining $200 million needed to meet the budget.

After an extensive Justice Department investigation, two former executives of the SLOC were indicted in the summer of 2000 on fraud, bribery for violating the Foreign Corrupt Practices Act, and conspiracy theories for orchestrating a wide-ranging bribery scheme of Olympic officials in order to secure the Winter 2000 games for Salt Lake City, Utah. Thomas Welch and David Johnson were the Salt Lake City Olympic Organizing Committee officials named in the indictment; and they were accused of paying more than $1 million in cash and bogus contracts to IOC officials in an effort to "buy" votes. Welch was the head of the committee of civic leaders that put together the city's bid for the winter Olympics, and Johnson was his deputy.

However, less than three months before the Games began, a federal judge dismissed all the charges. An internal IOC probe led to the dismissal of 10 IOC members. Nonetheless, the federal government appealed the judge's decision, and in April of 2003, a federal appeals court reinstated the case against Welch and Johnson, stating that the government deserved a chance to put the case before a jury. However, in December of 2003, another federal judge dismissed the criminal case against the two Salt Lake civic leaders. This judge, U.S. District Court Judge David Sam, was especially bitter to the federal government. He declared that in his 18 years on the federal bench, he had never seen a case so devoid of "criminal intent or evil purpose." The judge further stated that the evidence never met the legal standard for bribery, and that the case "offends my sense of justice." The judge formally acquitted the two men, which means the government cannot appeal again, because retrying them would amount to illegal "double jeopardy." The two men had faced up to 75 years in prison, although they probably would have received far less if actually convicted. Even if the case had reached a jury, the prosecution would have had a difficult time, since proof of evil intent or bad motive is an indispensable element to a case of bribery and fraud.

Case Summary and Discussion Questions

The saga of the Salt Lake City bribery case legal case, as well as the "scandal-plagued" Salt Lake City Winter Olympics, is now "history." Nonetheless, the Salt Lake City case is still a very illustrative and instructive one indeed for the legal, moral, cultural, and practical issues it raised. The authors, therefore, suggest that the Salt Lake City case be formulated as a case study for academic course work and corporate training programs. Accordingly, the authors recommend the use of the following questions for case analysis and discussion purposes:

1. Do you agree with the ultimate legal conclusion to the case? Do you believe there was sufficient evidence for a jury to conclude that "evil intent" and a "corrupt motive" were present?

2. Did the SLOC act in a moral manner pursuant to the ethical doctrines of Ethical Egoism, Ethical Relativism, Utilitarianism, and Kantian ethics? What was the relevant "society" for the purposes of Ethical Relativism? Was it global society, U.S. society, Utah society, Salt Lake City society, or IOC society? Why is the determination of the pertinent "society" critical to any Ethical Relativism analysis?
3. Did the companies that contributed to the SLOC organizing fund act in a socially responsible manner?
4. How could such a situation have been avoided by the SLOC and the IOC? Would corporate compliance programs, ethics training and ethics codes and corporate codes of conduct have helped?

Summary

This chapter presented and discussed an actual bribery prosecution and court case based on the Foreign Corrupt Practices Act. The authors reviewed the case of the Salt Lake City Olympic bribery scandal, which served to illustrate several legal, ethical, and practical issues relating to bribery and the FCPA. The chapter also provided discussion questions at the end of the case, which can be used for analytical, discussion, and training purposes. The next chapter will offer strategies and tactics and make recommendations as to how the global businessperson and his or her company can avoid legal liability pursuant to the FCPA.

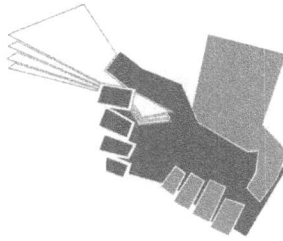

CHAPTER SEVEN

Management Strategies and Tactics

This chapter presents strategies and tactics and offers suggestions that the global executive, manager, and entrepreneur can use to avoid personal and company liability pursuant to the FCPA. In particular, corporate compliance programs and their relationship to the FCPA are discussed. Whistleblowing in the context of bribery is also addressed.

Corporate Compliance Programs and the FCPA

Legal commentators consistently stress that the "secret" to avoiding FCPA legal problems is a well-designed and fully executed FCPA compliance program (Bishop and Johnson, 2009; Dworsky, 2009). The major elements of such a compliance program are: 1) a corporate policy of adherence to the law and ethics; 2) education and training regarding the policy; 3) sufficient personnel to monitor compliance, including independent internal auditors and oversight committees; 4) appropriate contract provisions standard in all contracts to ensure legal compliance; 5) a reporting system for suspected violations, including provisions for the protection of "whistleblowers"; 6) explicit and specific disciplinary procedures; and 7) adequate record-keeping systems to ensure compliance with the FCPA (Bishop and Johnson, 2009). Of course, having a code of ethics and corporate compliance program are no guarantees of legal and ethical behavior. For example, in the aforementioned Daimler bribery settlement with the Justice Department, the *Miami Herald* reported that the company's board of directors over a decade ago had adopted a corporate integrity code, including specific anti-bribery provisions, but the problem was that the company failed to enforce it, and furthermore that company executives "actively resisted" it (Yost and Barrett, 2010, p. 2C).

When the government is investigating and considering whether to prosecute, important factors prosecutors will consider are whether the company has taken any remedial action, particularly creating a compliance program or improving a current one, as well as a company's rapid recognition of any flaws in its program, and its willingness to accept responsibility for its actions (Bishop and Johnson, 2009). To illustrate, in the Willbros Group case, the U.S. Justice Department agreed to defer criminal prosecution of the company pursuant to the Foreign Corrupt Practices Act for three years since the company cooperated with the investigation and had instituted compliance programs and efforts. If Willbros abides by the terms of the agreement, it will not be convicted of a felony (Eaton, 2008). Of course, if a company promises the government that it will institute anti-bribery policies and programs, then, obviously, by all means it should keep its promises and do so! To illustrate, in the $400 million bribery settlement between the British defense contractor, BAE, and the Justice Department, U.S. prosecutors also alleged that the company promised to institute anti-bribery programs, but then filed false documents to the U.S. government that it had implemented such programs when none existed (Michaels and Bryan-Low, 2010).

If a company is not sure whether the payment to a foreign government official will trigger government scrutiny, there is one tool that is available, called the Opinion Procedure Release process, whereby a firm can submit a set of facts for review by the Department of Justice and receive an opinion as to whether the government would take any enforcement action pursuant to the FCPA based on those facts (Lindsey, 2009). These "facts" must be real ones and represent a situation that a company actually is confronting; hypothetical scenarios cannot be submitted for review (Lindsey, 2009).Weinograd (2010) criticizes this Advisory Opinion Procedure as cumbersome, lengthy, and costly, and furthermore relates that "companies are also wary of the advisory opinion process because it exposes requestors to potential future liability" (p. 530). Specifically referring to the routine governmental action exception, Weinograd (2010) further points out that the Department of Justice can take up to 30 days to respond to an opinion request; and such a wait for approval of a facilitating and expediting payment might not be feasible practically and could be disastrous economically to the firm, particularly in the case of perishable goods. The fact that the government states that it will take no enforcement, however, is not entirely dispositive of the legal matter. Yet Dworsky (2009) explains that "if the government determines that a party's specified activities conform to the enforcement policy, any subsequent actions brought under the anti-bribery provisions is subject to a rebuttable presumption that the party's conduct complies with the FCPA" (pp. 687-88). Singer (2009) notes that the FCPA has produced "a surprisingly diminutive body of case law," and offers as a reasonable explanation the use by companies of this advisory process to receive opinions of the legal consequences of proposed actions (p. 292). Dworsky (2009) notes that the Department of Justice has issued 50 opinion letters.

Bribery and Whistleblowing

"Whistleblowing" can be defined as an attempt by a member of an organization to disclose what he or she believes to be wrongdoing in or by the organization, for example for the purposes herein, the payment of a bribe to a foreign government official. This discussion focuses on whistleblowing by employees of a corporation. "Wrongdoing" entails not only conduct or conditions that the employee believes are illegal, but also behavior that the employee considers to be immoral. Whistleblowing can be internal, that is, to those higher up in the corporate hierarchy; or it can be external, that is, to the government, such as a regulatory agency, to a public interest group, or to the media. A "whistleblower," of course, is the person, the employee, who attempts to make known the wrongdoing. He or she usually "blows the whistle" for right, as well as rightful, reasons; yet one should not always assume that the whistleblowing employee's motives are meritorious or that he or she is even correct as to the underlying premise of wrongdoing.

While there may exist federal and state statutes that protect public sector employees who "blow the whistle" from retaliation by their government employers, as well as specific statutes in the areas of civil rights, labor law, and health and safety law, that prohibit employers from taking retaliatory actions against employees who report statutory violations, there is no general federal statute, and little state law, extending similar protection to private sector employees, the vast majority of whom are employees "at-will" (and thus terminable for any or no good reason, and even a morally bad reason, but not an illegal reason). There does not yet exist a uniform corpus of whistleblower law to protect private sector employees. There is no general federal law protecting whistleblowers, though there are bills and proposals (see the National Whistleblower Center at www.whistleblowers.org for the latest information as to the laws and proposals to protect whistleblowers).

There is no whistleblower protection provision to the FCPA. However, the Sarbanes-Oxley Act (SOX) of 2002 does have a whistleblower protection provision. SOX, which applies to publicly traded companies, prohibits them from discharging, demoting, suspending, threatening, harassing, or otherwise discriminating against employees who provide to the government or assist in any government investigation regarding activities that the employee reasonably believes to be a violation of securities fraud laws. If the payment of a bribe could be construed as deceit or fraud against the shareholders, of if a bribe was misrepresented as a legitimate expense on the company's books, then arguably SOX and its protective provisions would apply to the whistleblowing employee. The whistleblowing employee would be protected under SOX if he or she disclosed the bribery internally or to a federal regulatory or law enforcement agency or to a member of Congress or a Congressional committee. The employee, however, is not protected if he or she makes the disclosure only to the media. In addition to SOX, there are some state whistleblower protection statutes, but only a relatively small number of truly comprehensive state statutes. Most of these contain strict reporting requirements, and, moreover, are strictly construed by the courts. Finally, there is a rather large, but loose, state-by-state collection of at times widely divergent, common law, "public policy" case formulations that may encompass whistleblowing protection for the at-will employee who discloses wrongdoing, such as bribery, that would violate the fundamental public policy of a state. The statutory and case law, of course, eventually will determine the legalities of a whistleblowing situation. The state whistleblower protection statutes that do exist usually only protect disclosures of actual legal violations by a company and by its employees. Therefore, reports of suspicious unfounded illegality are usually not protected, nor are disclosures of immoral and unethical conduct which are also not illegal. Moreover, the state statutes are uniform in that to be protected the whistleblowing must be made to a government agency or public official and not solely to the media or a public interest organization.

The issue arises, therefore, as to whether ethics extends any moral protection to private sector whistleblowing employees, especially in the corporate context. Whistleblowing presents an immediate dilemma as there is a clash between fundamental workplace values: the employee's moral right to free speech and the employee's duties of loyalty and confidentiality to his or her company or organization. It can be argued that employees have a moral obligation of loyalty and confidentiality. Yet it also can be argued persuasively that employees have a moral right to free speech, which at a minimum should include a right to "blow the whistle" on wrongful corporate activities. All these principles are moral ones; yet they clash in practice. What is the ethical solution to this problem?

Perhaps the solution is to qualify the general duties of loyalty and confidentiality. That is, to maintain generally that employees do owe a moral duty of loyalty and confidentiality to their employers, but also to maintain that this duty is not unlimited. The general duty can be superseded by special circumstances, such as when the employee not only has a moral free speech right, but also an obligation to "blow the whistle" in order to stop or prevent wrongdoing and harm.

An employee must follow proper guidelines in reporting corporate wrongdoing such as bribery. Whistleblower protection statutes that do exist will require certain procedures by the employee. Typically, he or she must first attempt to report the wrongdoing to his or her immediate supervisor. If, however, the supervisor is the person causing the problem, or is part of its cover-up, then the employee is allowed to circumvent the supervisor and proceed further "up the chain" in the corporate management hierarchy. In addition, if fully exhausting the internal corporate channels would give the wrongdoer(s) the time to destroy the evidence needed to document the wrong, then the whistleblower should not be required to proceed through the entire chain of command. Nonetheless, the employee who is contemplating whistleblowing is also advised to familiarize himself or herself with all available internal corporate channels and procedures for reporting wrongdoing as well as the requirements of any applicable whistleblower protection statutes. The employee also should seek to determine how other whistleblowing employees were treated by the company and what was done about the problems these employees reported. If employees were treated fairly and the problems rectified, then the employee should feel encouraged to proceed up the chain; if other employees were retaliated against, or if the problems were not corrected, then the employee is well advised to explore appropriate external whistleblowing contacts. If the wrongdoing involves illegal corporate actions, such as the payment of illegal bribes to foreign government officials, the proper external recipient of any disclosure is the governmental entity with jurisdiction over the subject matter, which would be either the Department of Justice or Securities and Exchange Commission.

An employee should not "blow the whistle" based on a mere

guess or speculation of wrongdoing, such as bribery, because such an action may harm innocent people. Also recall that some state whistleblower protection statutes will only protect an employee who reports an actual violation of the law. An employee, therefore, should obtain as much evidence and documentation as reasonably possible to substantiate and verify any allegation or wrongdoing. The employee should seek to gather sufficient evidence to allow others, internally or externally, to investigate the matter further; and should secure evidence that will stand up in a government proceeding. If it is not possible for the employee to secure this level of evidence, perhaps the employee can ascertain where and how additional evidence and documentation can be obtained. If, however, the employee possesses convincing reasons to believe that wrongdoing is occurring, he or she should disclose it, even if adequate documentation and evidence cannot be obtained. An employee simply may not be in a position to obtain this type or amount of information. What if the employee is able to obtain information, but only by engaging in illegal or immoral actions himself or herself? In such a case, the employee generally should refrain from personally acquiring the information, and instead inform others who would possess the necessary legal and moral authority to investigate. If the only way to obtain evidence is through illegal or immoral means, the employee must possess very good reasons to believe the wrongdoing is so severe and is causing such a substantial risk of harm to others that breaking the law and moral norms are unavoidably necessary.

Assuming that an employee is a "good" employee and thus intends to comply with the moral "law" and plans to "blow the whistle" on his or her employer's wrongdoing, such as bribery, the employee should nonetheless think carefully and plan accordingly. First, the employee should seek legal counsel to ascertain whether he or she is protected by a federal or state whistleblower protection statute. As noted, there is no whistleblower protection to the FCPA. There are whistleblower protection provisions in the Sarbanes-Oxley Act, which do extend to employees of publicly traded companies who make allegations of securities fraud, which might encompass bribery since the funds for the bribe have to come from some company account. Moreover, a few states do have general whistleblower protection acts, which protect to a limited degree private sector workers, and which certainly would encompass disclosing the illegal act of bribery. So, perhaps, the morally motivated, whistleblowing intending employee might be legally protected in certain states. If there is such a statute, it naturally would be incumbent on the employee to check the statute very carefully as to the particular state's requirements for legally protected whistleblowing. As previously noted, all state statutes will require that the predicate for protected whistleblowing be a legal violation; and furthermore most will require an actual, as opposed to a suspicion of a, legal violation by the employer. It should be noted that pursuant to SOX the whistleblowing employee need only have a reasonable belief in wrongdoing. Some statutes, furthermore, require that prior notice of the legal violation be given to the employer, and in some cases in writing, and also in certain cases that the employer be given a reasonable opportunity to correct the violation, such as the payment of bribes. Finally, as previously underscored, all whistleblower statutes – federal and state – will require that for the whistleblowing employee to be protected the disclosure must be made to an appropriate government agency or public sector official.

The occurrence of whistleblowing, especially external whistleblowing, ordinarily indicates a failure in a company's commitment to morality as well as a breakdown in its ethical structure and communication. If, however, a company has a legal compliance program, a code of ethics and conduct, an ethics or compliance department or officer, law and ethics training, and wrongdoing "hot lines," such a legally and morally committed company will enable its concerned employees to effectively raise any problems within the company through clearly defined channels, pursuant to explicit standards, and to empowered individuals. Regardless of any legal protections, such a company should have a provision in its code of ethics dealing explicitly with reporting suspected violations of the code, as well as other illegal or immoral actions, such as bribery. The provision should state that an employee who becomes aware of a violation, or believes that a violation may take place in the future, must report the matter. Ordinarily, this disclosure initially should be made to the employee's immediate supervisor. The code provision should then specify to whom else in the corporate hierarchy the employee must notify, including, of course, the ethics officer. It should state that the matter will be investigated promptly, thoroughly, and fairly, and that such reports will be treated confidentially. The code provision, finally, must state that any attempts at intimidation or retaliation against the reporting employee are strictly forbidden and consequently will be punished severely. It should be noted that under SOX the penalty for an employee, such as a manager or supervisor, who intentionally retaliates against a properly whistleblowing employee can be up a punishment of up to ten years in prison!

Recommendations for Managers and Entrepreneurs

While bribes are expected and accepted as a way of doing business in many countries, the FCPA prohibits and criminalizes certain payments made to foreign government officials. The international business person, moreover, must be concerned with any local laws that may prohibit payments to government officials. Of course, corrupt foreign government officials may not be concerned with the FCPA, the OECD, or for that matter their own local laws. In trying to advise the global manager and entrepreneur as to the legal meaning of the FCPA, one problem that surfaces is the fact that there is very little official legal guidance for companies that do want to comply with the statute. Lindsey (2009) explains that this paucity is because "there are few litigated cases because companies would rather settle bribery allegations with the government" (p. 975). Nevertheless, based on the current laws, cases, investigations, settlements, and prosecutions, as well as expert legal commentary, the authors in this section will offer the following guidelines, reflections, and suggestions.

A critical component pursuant to the FCPA to a legal classification of a payment as a bribe is the intent, purpose, or aim of the person making the payment to the foreign government official. The FCPA does not prohibit all transfers of anything of value to foreign officials; rather what is outlawed is the payment with the corrupt motive to receive some type of preferential business treatment. Weinograd (2010) explains that criminal intent could be inferred when: 1) payments are intended to change discretionary decision-making in order to increase a company's business; 2) payments that are "unusually large" compared to the government action performed; 3) payments that "directly affect competition in contracts, for instance, where the recipient controls the payor's future business with the government"; and 4) payments for services that the company was not entitled to (pp. 518-19). The requisite "evil mind" (or *mens rea* or "scienter" under the old common law) must be to make the payment with the intent of wrongfully directing business to oneself or one's company or to wrongfully retain business. Dworsky (2009) relates three instances where a jury could infer corrupt intent: 1) a close temporal relationship between the gift or payment and subsequent approval of a contract by the foreign official; 2) a close relationship between the recipient of the gift and the government official; and 3) the misclassification of a gift as a "commission" in the records of the company. The improper payment to the foreign official can be direct or it can be a separate indirect transaction, for example, a donation to a favored charity or organization, admission into a school, or employment of a third party (Bishop and Johnson, 2009). In the Salt Lake City case, the government felt that all the preceding separate transactions were sufficient evidence of "corrupt" motive. Regarding the "knowing" requirement, Dworsky (2009) gives some basic and very practical advice: "The 'knowing' standard in the anti-bribery provisions is intended to capture corporate officials who fail to take action when reasonable signs of a FCPA violation arise" (pp. 682-83).

Juries are allowed to infer intent – bad or otherwise - from the facts and circumstances of a case; that is, "inferential evidence" is permissible. For example, hiding or destroying potential evidence and otherwise hindering a government investigation are the actions of an "evil" person or company. So, in the Control Components case reported by the *Wall Street Journal*, the paper noted that the government's indictment specifically accused one former employee of the firm of "flushing incriminating documents down a ladies room toilet" (Searcy, 2009, p. A4). Moreover, in that case, the newspaper also reported that the company officials used code words to hide the bribes by referring to them as "flowers"; and also tried to hide the identity of the bribe recipients in emails by referring to them as a "friend in camp," that is, "friendly" government officials at various power plants who could be bribed (Searcy, 2009). Bishop and Johnson (2009) relate the following "red flags" of bad intent: 1) the involvement of shell companies in the transaction, especially if located offshore; 2) the involvement of government officials in an unofficial capacity, for example, as the owner of a company, a recommender of the company, or as the relative of someone involved with the transaction (p. 27). The *Wall Street Journal* noted in 2010 that Britain's BAE Systems, PLC reached a settlement of more than $400 million with the U.S. Justice Department based on allegations that it used shell companies and "secretive offshore entities" to conceal improper payments to foreign government officials to obtain defense contracts (Michaels and Bryan-Low, 2010, p. B6). In the 2010 Daimler settlement with the Justice Department for $185 million, the *Wall Street Journal* reported that in addition to the secret off-shore accounts to fund the bribes, the company classified the bribes as "commissions," "special discounts," and a German term that translates into "useful or necessary payments" (Fuhrmans and Catan, 2010, p. B2).

Dworsky (2009) lists other bribery "red flags": 1) requests by the foreign official that the company will provide false documentation; and 2) the size of the "commission" compared to the services performed by the foreign government official. Kramer (2002) relates that one common bribery scheme occurs when:

> A contractor might 'rent' property owned by a project official for the duration of the project (The contractor pays money to a project official to 'rent' office space but is actually making bribe payments. Often the space is never occupied). However, once the contract is awarded and the contractor has access to a steady

source of funds, a monetary kickback is, of course, the most common method of payment (pp. 24-25).

The problem with this scheme from a legal standpoint arises when the office space is not occupied, since the "dummy" office is evidence indicating that the parties possessed a wrongful intent to use the office as a device to make improper payments. Johnstone (2008) offers three hypothetical examples of payments that could cause legal problems due to an inference of corrupt motive being made: 1) inviting a government official and his/her spouse to discuss business opportunities with the vice-president of sales in Hawaii; 2) giving foreign officials a cash stipend to cover travel and meal expenses when visiting the company's headquarters; and 3) a foreign official agreeing to go to dinner but then requesting that his or her name not be included in any expense account forms (p. 645). In these situations, the payments "look, smell, and feel" more like illegal bribes than legitimate payments. In the Salt Lake City case, the federal jury may have been willing to find the requisite bad intent; but, as noted, the judge disagreed, dismissing the case with prejudice by formally acquitting the SLOC principals. The case is significant because judges rarely supersede juries and almost never on an issue of intent, which has long been regarded in Anglo-American law as a typical "question of fact" for the jury to determine.

Bishop and Johnson (2009) emphasize that each and every payment to a foreign official must have an identifiable purpose and naturally a legitimate one. Johnstone (2008) also advises to never hide, lose, or destroy records since "the U.S. government is likely to assume the worst about suspiciously lost or destroyed records, particularly where the shoddy recordkeeping or records destruction campaign relates uniquely to FCPA-relevant business matters" (p. 646).

As underscored, not all payments to foreign government officials are prohibited by the FCPA. Gifts to foreign government officials are not necessarily illegal. A legal problem will arise when a gift is given with a corrupt motive to gain some type of business advantage from the foreign government official. Yet to complicate matters, gift-giving is an established part of doing business in some cultures. Gift-giving may be viewed as a customary practice to show hospitality, thanks, and to create and maintain business good will. Actually, not giving gifts in some cultures can be seen as a very inappropriate act. The giving of "greeting," hospitality, or seasonal gifts, which is very common in certain cultures, emerges as a major problem area of the law. Admittedly, given the broad wording of the FCPA, it can be difficult to ascertain whether a gift is a legal gratuity or an illegal bribe in a given situation. Gifts are definitely a "gray" area under the law. For example, the *Wall Street Journal* informally sampled corporate attorneys and asked "whether buying a foreign official a $100 dinner could get them into trouble"; and the response was that they "still don't know" (Searcy, 2009, p. A13). One legal commentator advised that to be legal, "gifts should be modest, never involve cash payments, and be given only at culturally appropriate times" (Johnstone, 2008, p. 643). Gifts to charities can also cause legal problems. Johnstone (2008) cites an example where the U.S. government penalized a U.S. pharmaceutical company $500,000 for donating $76,000 to a Polish charity. The problem was that the president of the charity was also a government official, the director of regional governmental health authority, and the government contended the "donation" was intended to influence the director's pharmaceutical purchasing decisions. Consequently, Johnstone (2008) counsels the business community to "be vigilant for more creative schemes designed to disguise inappropriate payments" (p. 645). Bishop and Johnson (2009) advise that gifts be "customary" as well as be properly recorded by the gift-giving company. Dworsky (2009, n83) further advises that gifts be "nominal," as well as bestowed as a "courtesy, a token or regard of esteem, or in return for hospitality." Key factors in determining intent, according to Dworsky (2009), are the value of the gift in the context of the situation, local customs and business practices, as well as the laws and regulations of the host country. In the Salt Lake City case, the government believed that the nature and extent of the gifts "crossed the line" into illegal bribe payments, though the federal judge ultimately disagreed.

Facilitating and expediting payments for routine governmental actions are generally permissible pursuant to the FCPA. As succinctly explained by Weinograd (2010): "Congress did not intend to criminalize payments that merely hastened the inevitable" (p. 517). It is important to point out that there is no dollar limit in the statute or guidance as to what might constitute a permissible, small-scale, facilitating and expediting payment. Weinograd (2010) thus explains that "because the statute focuses on payor intent and payment purpose, its plain language suggests that even large bribes designed to solicit routine government action do not give rise to criminal liability" (p. 516). The FCPA does not explicitly limit the size of facilitating and expediting payments. Weinograd (2010) also reports that in the past the U.S. Congress has rejected the imposition of a dollar cap on facilitating and expediting payments, because "by using a cap to define bribery, Congress might create a floor price for doing business abroad. Corrupt officials would persistently demand the exact amount of the threshold" (p. 546). Nonetheless, legal commentators counsel that such payments should be small gratuities, modest, and a common occurrence in the host country, as well as legal there (Bishop and Johnson, 2009). Dworsky (2009) notes that there is no statutory limit on the amount of such payments, but nonetheless relates that "grease" payments that have been allowed have been less than $1000. The *Wall Street Journal* (Searcy, 2009) noted that the U.S. "Justice Department has typically targeted companies that have paid a long trail of high-dollar bribes over several years" (p. A4). Yet the paper also noted that since these types of payments must be recorded on a company's books and records, if there are reported numerous facilitating and expediting payments, a company will bring upon itself greater scrutiny of its international business practices (Searcy, 2009). Weinograd (2010) also underscored that the routine government action exception is not a defense to accounting omissions or irregularities; and thus a company must carefully document any facilitating and expediting payments on its books. It is also important for the global business person to ascertain whether such payments are permissible under the law of the host country. For example, South Korea, Canada, and New Zealand, like the U.S., permit such payments, but many countries do not (Searcy, 2009). Weinograd (2010) notes that critics of the FCPA have condemned the facilitating and expediting exception for undermining the moral basis of the anti-bribery provisions in the law by legislatively creating a "fissure" in the law's foundation "enabling corporations to use petty bribes in a way that undermines the Act's fundamental anti-corruption purpose" (p. 511). Moreover, the *Wall Street Journal* reported that there is a movement in the Organization for Economic Cooperation and Development (OECD) to ban these types of "routine" payments since, according to the OECD, they are "corrosive...particularly on economic development and the rule of law" (Searcy, 2009, p. A4).

Reasonable, legitimate, and *bona fide* payments to foreign officials for travel, meals, and lodging are permissible if the trip is related to the demonstration or explanation of a product or service. Dworsky (2009, n83) points to several instances where the government gave approval, including transportation costs, meals, and lodging, as well as seminar fees and "promotional expenses" for visiting foreign government officials. One legal commentator advised that travel and meals for foreign officials "should not be lavish and may occur only for legitimate purposes – and not in an effort to coerce or reward a foreign official for using his or her influence to funnel business to your company" (Johnstone, 2008, p. 643). However, in the Salt Lake City case, the Justice Department, obviously, felt that the Salt Lake Organizing Committee went too far and "crossed the line" into illegal bribe "territory." A federal jury may have agreed that the expenditures were not reasonable and not legitimate; but, as noted, the federal judge disagreed with the government and a jury did not have that opportunity. More recently, the *Wall Street Journal* (Searcy, 2009) reported that in 2007 the Justice Department settled charges against the telecommunications company, Lucent Technologies, Inc., for paying millions of dollars in travel expenses to about 1000 Chinese foreign government officials for trips to Disney World, Las Vegas, and other tourist destinations. The Chinese officials worked for state-controlled telephone companies. Lucent characterized the trips as "factory tours"; Lucent admitted wrongful conduct and paid $2.5 million in fines. Kramer

(2002) relates that "corruption schemes sometimes begin with an official demanding or offering relatively small gifts, lavish entertainment, paid travel, or paid study tours or educational expenses for the official's children (a common scheme)" (p. 24). Johnstone (2008) cautions that there is no real guidance in the FCPA as "how much fun is too much fun"; nevertheless, he advises that "a safe rule of thumb is that leisure time should make up no more than 25 percent of company-sponsored travel" (p. 646).

Also permissible under the FCPA are the payments of required fees to government officials so long as the payments are set forth in the written laws or regulations of the foreign state. To illustrate, in one Florida case reported by the *Miami Herald* (Christensen, 2008), a federal lawsuit arose over the payments by a U.S. company to Jordanian government officials in order to obtain an "exclusive letter" from the Jordanian officials for the U.S. firm to transport fuel across Jordan to Iraq. Companies without this letter were not allowed to bid on lucrative government transport contracts. The key issue in the case is whether the payment was an illegal bribe to Jordanian government officials or "merely" a required government fee to transport military fuel through Jordan. The U.S. company contends that the fee was paid to an official agency of the Jordanian state, that the fee was properly documented, the fee was required by the foreign government; and a Jordanian government official stated that the fee arrangement was proper (Christensen, 2008).

When doing business globally, it is a customary, acceptable, as well as prudent practice to engage local representatives to deal with the government bureaucracy and customs of the foreign county. However, when dealing with third-party agents, particularly from the host country, a company must be very careful since under the law a company's legal obligations extend by virtue of agency law, especially the vicarious liability doctrine, as well as the FCPA, to those third parties doing business for the company at its direction or authorization, or with its knowledge. As noted, agents from the host country can provide very valuable local knowledge, perspectives, and networking connections; they know how to "navigate" through the local "waters"; yet they may be ignorant of or indifferent to U.S. law.

Bishop and Johnson (2009) underscore that the use of foreign agents is one of the "deadliest traps" in the FCPA (p. 27). They thus recommend that "foreign agents must be carefully selected, screened and supervised" (Bishop and Johnson, 2009, p. 27). At a minimum, Johnstone (2008) recommends complete background checks and strict FCPA compliance provisions in the contracts between the company and the agents. Johnstone (2008) also points to three common "red flags" that should prompt further investigation into the retaining of the agent: 1) requests for cash payments or reimbursement for undocumented expenses; 2) requests to sub-contract work to third parties and intermediaries; and 3) refusals to provide references and detailed descriptions of business practices (p. 645). Bishop and Johnson (2009) point out that another "red flag" will be the request by the foreign agent for a sizeable "commission," because "it is quite possible that a part will end up as a payoff to a foreign government official" (p. 27). Accordingly, they counsel that "any agreements with a foreign agent should be documented in detail, describing the services to be performed and forbidding any conduct that would be considered a violation of the FCPA" (Bishop and Johnson, 2009, p. 27). Dworsky (2009) states that appropriate contract provisions can help to prevent FCPA violations, and accordingly recommends that contracts clearly state the identity of third party agents or business parties, an acknowledgment that these local parties are aware of the FCPA, an agreement to abide by the company's policy of adherence to the FCPA, and a stated willingness to have their expenses and invoices audited by the company. Dworsky (2009) explains that compliance policies and contract provisions will reduce the chance of success if an employee or agent claims that he or she merely inadvertently violated the FCPA. Furthermore, "the adoption of an appropriate contractual measure can reduce the risk of a violation and can be used as evidence of intent to comply with the FCPA" (Dworsky, 2009, p. 696).

One bit of advice that the authors frequently hear and see is to "let the locals deal with the locals," that is, let the local nationals deal with the local government officials since the "locals" know the "system" and any "fees" that have to be paid. Another suggestion is for the U.S. business person to seek out the counsel in the U.S. Chamber of Commerce. Such Chambers exist in almost every country in the world; and there one can find American "ex-pats" who live in the country and who know how to accomplish business objectives. A business person could also contact the U.S. embassy or a consulate for assistance; yet should be mindful that these U.S. government entities must adhere to official government policy, and thus "stick to the party line" (Allen, 2009). Kramer (2002) explains that:

> More sophisticated parties involved with larger projects conceal bribes as payment to a local 'agent' or subcontractor who fronts for a project official. This allows the contractor to deduct the payment, and if the bribes are later discovered, it enables him to deny knowledge of intent. In some cases, the parties will conceal bribes by the paying the agent or retaining the subcontractor through an affiliate or subsidiary, which might be located halfway around the world (p. 25).

Obviously, these bribery practices are unethical as well as very risky legal tactics. One point is evident about the FCPA. It is a very vague statute; and intentionally vague according to one legal commentator (Johnstone, 2008). As a result, the U.S. government possesses a great deal of discretionary enforcement power. Weinograd (2010) similarly states that the statute is "riddled with ambiguity," and as a result, "corporations are left...to decipher the Act's vague language within a vacuum of textual, judicial, and regulatory guidance" (p. 511). Weinograd (2010) also underscores the ambiguity of the statute and the lack of definitive judicial and agency opinions. As a result, Weinograd (2010) asserts that the Department of Justice and the Securities and Exchange Commission "clearly enjoy enormous prosecutorial discretion. Wielding the broadsword of criminal sanctions, these agencies are free to interpret the FCPA equivocal language as they see fit" (p. 525). Another practical and related consequence of such a broadly worded criminal law statute, combined with a now heightened enforcement environment, is that the FCPA, in the words of the *Wall Street Journal*, "is spawning an army of consultants, some of whom once prosecuted bribery cases for Justice Department, who offer to interpret the gray areas" (Searcey, 2009, p. A1). The retaining of a specialized and knowledgeable international business law attorney to guide a company through the maze of complex U.S. and foreign anti-corruption laws, as well as to establish appropriate policies, controls, and training, is highly recommended by the authors of this work. Retaining legal counsel always provides evidence of good faith and due diligence and demonstrates a good intent to comply with the law.

Regardless of "local" advice and not withstanding any consultant's expert counsel, it is always prudent, in international business dealings and otherwise, to take heed of the very old, and true, maxim – "Be good, but if you can't be good, be careful." One case will plainly illustrate this maxim. The *Miami Herald* (Oppenheimer, 2000) reported on one bribery case in the mid-1990's involving IBM, where IBM executives in Argentina were accused of bribing government officials to secure a $250 million contract with an entity of the Argentine government. IBM defended itself by saying that executives at the company's New York headquarters did not know of the bribes, and were in fact deceived by the company's Argentine managers. The U.S. Justice Department instituted an investigation to determine if the FCPA was violated, and the U.S. government requested that the Argentine government conduct an investigation. The U.S. investigation indicated that IBM executives in New York had closely supervised the general aspects of the contract; yet the IBM executives denied that they were aware of the existence of a "shell company" for the project, which was an IBM sub-contractor, but existed only "on paper" and never performed any real work other than purportedly paying bribes to the Argentine government officials. However, the investigations suffered what the *Miami Herald* deemed a "major blow" when a key witness, the executive for the alleged shell company in Argentina, was found dead, hanging from an electricity pole, with a newspaper clipping about the IBM case stuck in his mouth. The *Miami Herald* reported that an Argentine police source concluded that the executive's death was a suicide (Oppenheimer, 2000, p. 2E).

Summary

This chapter presented strategies and tactics and offered suggestions that the global executive, manager, and entrepreneur can use to avoid personal and company liability pursuant to the FCPA. In particular, corporate compliance programs and their relationship to the FCPA were discussed. The next chapter provides a brief summary and conclusion to the book as well as some public affairs and public relation strategies followed by a series of case problems and a glossary of key terms.

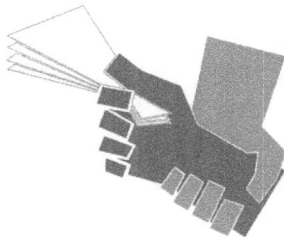

CHAPTER EIGHT

CONCLUSION AND CASE DILEMMAS

This final chapter provides a brief summary and some final thoughts along with a strategy for public affairs and public relations in order to effectively deal with legal and ethical challenges. Then the chapter provides a number of different dilemmas that employees and managers of a multinational firms or even small firms might face when there are doing business across borders. These case problems or dilemmas can be used for discussions, debates, and assessment purposes to help learners better understand what they might face in international dealings. Finally, a glossary of key terms is presented.

Concluding Thoughts

Bribery and other forms of corruption can pose huge obstacles to a country's advancement. As such, each country and each company should have a comprehensive anti-corruption campaign. Bribery can be a "hidden tax" that impedes economic growth, erodes respect for law, order, and justice, and destroys people's trust in their government officials, institutions, and government. Bribery is also a serious legal wrong pursuant to the Foreign Corrupt Practices Act as well as other foreign laws and international agreements. The U.S. government, moreover, is now more aggressively enforcing the FCPA, and receiving greater cooperation by foreign governments too. There clearly has been in recent years a marked increase in government investigation and enforcement activity. The FCPA has emerged as one of the most significant legal issues in international business and commerce. For all these reasons, therefore, any astute business person that is contemplating expanding into foreign markets must have some basic knowledge of the FCPA and other anti-corruption laws. To ignore or to downplay this law will place a company and its personnel at serious risk of lengthy and costly investigations as well as potentially large fines and long prison sentences. FCPA anti-bribery compliance programs and practices and the exercise of due diligence can be expensive and time-consuming, but efforts to act in a legal and ethical manner will save the business time, effort, and money in the long-term and will avoid criminal and civil sanctions and a blemished reputation.

Of course, it is best when any efforts toward ethical behaviors and legal compliance are part of a comprehensive anti-corruption strategy to create awareness of existing laws and moral standards and their enforcement. Figure 1 presents some of the elements that should be included in a comprehensive model for the creation and enforcement of an effective anti-corruption program (Mujtaba, 2010c). Any effective anti-corruption model, at the government or corporate level, should include education and training, transparency of record keeping and contracts, disciplinary actions for violations of legal and ethical standards, and regular auditing or inspections of major contracts to make sure everyone is in compliance with the rules and policies.

As part of a comprehensive anti-bribery and anti-corruption program, a country's citizens as well as political and business leaders should become "ethical allies" by reporting cases of bribery and not tolerating it in order to have a business culture where people from around the world would want to come for pleasure, business, and investment opportunities. Ethical allies are those individuals who refuse to pay bribes and simultaneously discourage others from expecting kickbacks or giving bribes to unfairly influence others (Mujtaba, 2010c). Ethical allies say something when they see someone giving a bribe, or if they see a situation that looks like a bribe is about to take place, they say something to discourage any corrupt actions. As mentioned by Dale Carnegie, "Most of the important things in the world have been accomplished by people who have kept on trying when there seemed to be no hope at all." All business and political leaders as well as every citizen in the community must continue to work as ethical allies to create a just and fair political system and business environment for everyone.

Figure 1 – Anti-Corruption Campaign Model

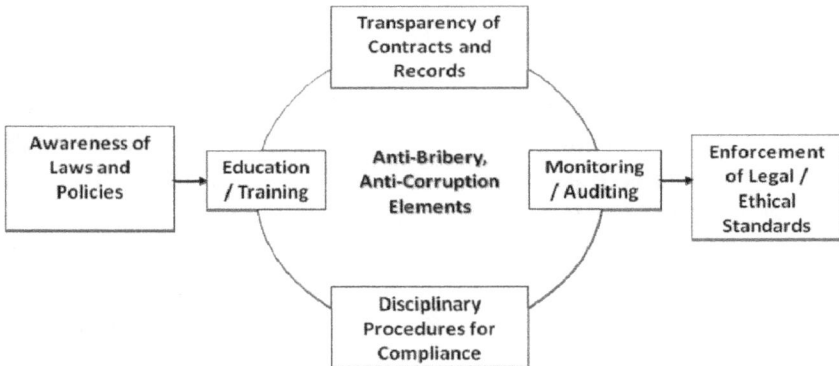

Public Affairs and Public Relations

According to Rajib N. Sanyal (2006, p. 478), a public affairs strategy is usually adopted by multinational companies to deal with the public and governmental agencies regarding business affairs, including the accusations of bribery, which can be a huge media relations problem, as well as a legal one, in today's global workplace. Large multinational companies usually have a public affairs and public relations department that handles all the tasks associated with external interface and liaison. The tasks include handling legal, political, and public relations issues that may arise in both the domestic and host countries.

Each firm is likely to face some form a crisis sooner or later, and implications or accusations of corruption or bribery certainly can be one of them (Mujtaba, 2010d)[3]. As such, firms should be prepared to effectively deal with such challenges. An effective public affairs strategy can help the organization communicate its perspective while shedding a positive light on the organization in question. Accordingly, organizations should have experts and professionals who are dedicated to this public affairs responsibility. These professionals should be able to assess the environment, including the local, legal, and the international perspectives of the business environment. These public affairs professionals must plan quickly using effective communication skills. Besides good communication skills, public affairs professionals must also have current knowledge of how the public affairs efforts can affect the organization economically both in the short term as well as in the long term. These professionals should also have good negotiation capabilities, as well as a firm understanding of the social ramifications of the organization's policy (Sanyal, 2006, p. 478).

Of course, ethics and social responsibility play a critical role in how organizations set and implement their public affairs strategy. As commonly known, "Ethics refers to what is good and bad in the context of what is moral duty and obligation" (Sanyal, 2006, p. 450). Unfortunately, many organizations have had executives that have acted in morally questionable manners. As stated by Sanyal, white-collar crimes, manufacturing, marketing, or selling materials that have

---

[3] Presentation at the *2nd International Conference of South Asia Chapter of AGBA*. July 18-23, 2010. COMSATS Institute of Information Technology. Bhurban, Pakistan.

been found harmful in countries whose legislation has not yet addressed them, discriminatory employment practices, "fudging" the books, receiving or giving bribes, as well as leveraging corporate funds as a way to gain political favor, are some of the ways in which corporate ethics have been questionable in nature (2006, p. 450). It should be noted that some countries do not publicize such issues as readily as is done in the developed societies, such as the United States, Canada, or many European countries (Sanyal, 2006, p. 451) In some instances, such as bribery cases of political and high-ranking business leaders and government officials, the ethical dilemmas faced by an organization are publicized as a way to shame the organization into acting in a more ethically desirable way. Sometimes this is done by public outrage, legislation, prosecutions, lawsuits, or stakeholder demand in order to force firms toward socially desirable conduct and socially responsible contributions in the community.

Social responsibility generally means that an organization ought to pursue its goal of profitability while embarking in practices that are also cognizant of the society in which it does business. In an international context, this means remaining mindful of the environments both of the local country and the organization's home country (Sanyal, 2006, p. 453). Different nations might emphasize social responsibility according to their own customs and norms. For example, in Japan, *Kyosei* is the "philosophy of corporate social responsibility," and it is defined "a spirit of cooperation" (Sanyal, 2006, p. 470). Generally speaking, according to Sanyal, "A firm that practices Kyosei establishes harmonious relationships with its customers, suppliers, competitors,…governments,…and the natural environment" (2006, p. 470). This is a principle that has been proved true throughout many years of organizational success in Japan, and the world is paying attention. Organizations are making it the principal a part of their training, and clearly educational institutions are teaching it in an effort to breed a new generation of future business leaders, entrepreneurs, and executives that will understand and consistently practice it; thus creating a new generation of the workforce that will conduct business in a more socially responsible way.

There are several steps an organization can take to alleviate a negative public image while keeping in line with the theme of corporate legal and ethical behavior and corporate social responsibility. According to Sanyal (2006), these steps can include improving working conditions, ceasing improper operations and misconduct, establishing social welfare projects, working with advocacy groups, labeling products, obtaining certification of proper conduct, engaging in ethics training, and creating external auditing committees to monitor the actions of the firm to ensure legal and ethical behavior (pp. 476-77). Of course, for most businesses, ceasing operations cannot be an effective option as they must survive and remain competitive. Improving working conditions and creating a more ethical environment for decision-making are actions that could be helpful in creating a positive public affairs strategy. Establishing social welfare projects and working with advocacy groups are steps that are extremely helpful in any organizations development of a public affairs strategy. Healthy relationships in these arenas lead to positive press, the opportunity for organizations to give back to the communities in which they do business, and are generally good exercises in social responsibility. As an added bonus, these relationships often lead to tax cuts and increased profits as well (Campbell, 2009). Of course, in the cases of blatant bribery, it is clear that no organization would always be perceived in a positive light; however, it is possible that the proper public affairs and public relations strategies can reduce the negative publicity and ameliorate the legal fines imposed on an organization.

It is clear that an effective public affairs strategy is necessary for any company, domestic, national, or multi-national, as their managers may "have to respond to crises, explain the firms conduct, and work to deflect negative publicity" (Sanyal, p. 478). In cases of bribery scandals, what is important is that the company creates a public affairs strategy that will be in the best interest of the company and its stakeholders, while also decreasing the negative attention the firm is receiving. "Failure to make correct choices can cost the firm in many ways: expensive legal settlements or criminal penalties, damaging media publicity, loss of key executive or restrictions on business activities, and denial of access to markets and contracts." (Sanyal, p. 450). Perhaps one of the first steps in the public affairs strategy should be the conducting of a "relationship analysis" and environmental scanning. Sanyal (2006, p. 470) indicates that such an analysis should include the following:

- Identifying the stakeholders that will be affected by a decision and the nature of their interests.
- Evaluating the level of responsibilities and obligations to each of these stakeholders.
- Relying on facts and information as much as possible.
- Evaluating all options.
- Considering ethical issues in addition to economic, political, managerial, and legal consequences.
- Distinguishing clearly between culturally determined behaviors and an individual's personality and behavior.
- Evaluating the impact of a decision on an individual manager's personal value system.

This assessment or relationship analysis will allow the firm's leaders and managers to understand what responsibilities they hold and what might be the best decision for the company. Firms and managers need to understand what their obligations are to all their stakeholders, including the local community and society as a whole, as well what the possible consequences might be when implementing different strategies. Of course, the firm dealing with a bribery scandal is going to need to look at whether it wants to deal with the problem or ignore it; but because of the detrimental effects from negative bribery publicity as well as the legal sanctions can have on the company, the last thing they should do is ignore it. The Crisis Response Option Model (Sanyal, p. 473) explains four possible strategies a company can choose from when dealing with a legal and social responsibility crisis, and they include:

- *Reaction* - the firm denies that the problem exists, or if it does, it is not the organization's fault.

- *Defense* - the firm seeks to explain the problem in legalistic terms and usually mounts a vigorous public relations campaign to project its "story."
- *Accommodation* - the firm is compelled to assume some responsibilities, usually by various interest groups or the government.
- *Proactive* - the firm on its own takes initiative to resolve the problem. The firm will acknowledge the problems and go about correcting it without delay and without prodding from various stakeholders.

One good strategy in the case of obvious bribery would be to assume responsibility for the problem and create a procedures and policies to prevent this wrongful act from happening in the future. Another step in this strategy is to take some of the negative attention off the company and show the public the good the company does and has done. Everything that the company does to "give back" to the community in which the firm is located or does business should be high-lighted. The firm needs to point out all the positive things it is doing for the community and society so the public can see the "bigger picture," and thus perceive how the company is very active and socially responsible in the community. A multinational company should always proactively respond to any negative publicity that bribery scandals bring by creating proper procedures for future decisions and penalizing those involved in illegal and unethical behaviors.

In summary, the executives, managers, and employees are responsible for properly responding to a crisis, deflecting negative publicity, and explaining company conduct to customers, employees, external audit committees, government officials, and other stakeholders. The skills required by public affairs department personnel include understanding the political climate, awareness of issues that engage advocacy groups, information gathering and analysis, and communication and negotiation skills. Information is gathered from various sources, such as economists, pollsters, sociologists, psychologists, and political scientists. The public affairs personnel can and must use this information and their professional skills and expertise to ensure that the company's goals are matched with the public interest in a legal, ethical, and socially acceptable way.

Case Problems

This final section to the book presents a series of case problems involving payments to foreign officials which might bring about legal liability for making bribes pursuant to the FCPA. These legal and ethical dilemmas can be used for analytical as well as discussion and training purposes. They are based on actual or "real-life" "bribery" scenarios. Some of these payments might be illegal bribes and some could be quite legal payments to foreign officials. There are no definitive answers due to the vague nature of the FCPA and the paucity of legal decisions interpreting the statute. The intent of the authors is to raise the awareness of the readers as to bribery situations they may encounter in doing business globally; and then for the readers to use the legal and ethical principles and professional commentary and opinion they learned in the book to make well-reasoned decisions as to the legality and morality of these payments. Yet whether the U.S. government agrees with the readers' legal conclusions is another matter indeed! Nevertheless, working with these case problems and dilemmas will help the readers recognize legal issues in international business and, with the use of the legal principles and recommendations learned in the book, to make some reasoned determinations as to the legality of certain payments. Moreover, the use of these case problems will alert the international business person to promptly call in expert legal counsel so as to avoid personal and company liability, particularly when a payment to a foreign official appears questionable or problematical. As the old maxim says: "To be forewarned is to be forearmed"!

Legal and Ethical Dilemmas

1. *The Commission.* A company is the low bidder on a multi-million dollar contract with a foreign government. To secure the contract is very important to the firm's survival as well as a manager's position and advancement in the company. The contract is looked upon favorably by the foreign government, and is about to be awarded, when the key government official involved requests a "commission" of $100,000. If this commission is not paid, the foreign official tells the manager that he "regrets" that the contract will go to a competitor. The manager pays the "commission" and the contract is obtained. Do you agree with the payment of this "commission" to the official? Why or why not?

2. *The Scholarship Fund.* A delegation of foreign government officials is visiting a company to view its facilities, observe its processes, and to meet key personnel. They are very seriously considering the company for a very large contract. In addition to, and separate from, the contract provisions, they request as a "socially responsible" act the creation of a $400,000 educational scholarship fund, specifically to be used by 13 people, including several relatives of the foreign government officials. This good will "gesture," they relate, will cause them to look very favorably on the company's contract offer. The company creates the "scholarship." The contract is obtained. Do you agree with the decision to create this scholarship fund? Why or why not

3. *The Medical Surgeries.* A very important foreign government official is visiting a company to discuss a contract offer that the firm has made with the official's government. The approval of the foreign government official is critical to securing the contract. The foreign government official asks as a "humanitarian" act that the company pay for the official's knee surgery as well as for his wife's cosmetic surgery while they are in the country. The amounts involved are inconsequential compared to the value of the contract with the foreign government to the company. The

company arranges to have these medical services provided. The official approves the contract. Do you agree with the payment for these surgeries? Why or why not?

4. *The Gifts.* A very important foreign government official is visiting a company to view its facilities, meet key company representatives, and to discuss an offer the company has made to the official's government. The meeting with the foreign government official has gone very well, and he appears disposed to recommend that his government accept the firm's offer. When the official returns home he finds that the company had made an unsolicited gift to him of two fancy "replica" shotguns and two pure-bred puppies. The official recommends the company. Do you agree with the making of these gifts? Why or why not?

5. *The Real Estate Deal.* A foreign government official whose approval is critical to the awarding of a very large contract with his government to a company requests an "extra-contractual" payment of $65,000 to "firmly" secure his approval. Since to pay this amount directly appears problematical, a representative of the company suggests that the company "orchestrate" a quick real estate venture, which in and of itself would be quite legal, involving the foreign official, so that he can make a quick, risk-free, turn-a-round profit of about the amount she requested. The foreign official agrees to this land deal. The company sets up this land deal. The foreign official approves the contract. Do you agree with the decision to set up this land deal? Why or why not?

6. *The Travel Layover.* A high-level foreign government official along with his wife and children are coming to the country to view a company's facilities and to meet with key personnel to discuss a contract offer the company has made to his government. The contract would be a very large one and very important to the success of the firm. The company is paying for their transportation, lodging, and meals. However, there are no direct flights from the foreign official's home country and the city where

the company's manufacturing facilities are located. The foreign official consequently will have to change planes in Paris. He requests that in order to relieve his "jet lag," so that he will be "fresh" and "receptive" to the company's proposals, that he and his family spend a week in Paris, as a "little layover," while in transit to the company's home city, with this additional part to the trip also to be paid at the company's expense. The company agrees to pay for all the travel. The official recommends the company for the contract. Do you agree with the decision to provide the foreign official and his family with this travel, including the additional Paris "layover"? Why or why not?

7. *The "To-Go" Bag.* The manager of a company has completed negotiations with a very high-level government official whose final approval is necessary for the contract between her company and the official's government. The contract is for a massive, multi-billion project. Securing this huge contract is absolutely critical to the company, and actually without it the company would face bankruptcy. The foreign government official is about to sign, but firsts request his "courtesy" "To-Go" bag. The manager is uncertain as to what this is, until one of her local agents informs her that a "To-Go" bag is a large, thatched, woven, colorful bag, which is a local handicraft, and which the foreign official expects, and will demand, to be filled with U.S. currency, specifically $100 bills. The manager "roughly" calculates that to fill the bag and make this payment to the foreign official would take several hundred thousand dollars. Her local agent says that this "To-Go" bag is a customary way of doing business in his country for these types of very large contracts with very high-level officials. Without this payment, the company will not get the contract. The manager gets the cash, makes the payment, and the company gets the contract. Do you agree with the decision to fill the "To-Go" bag with cash and give it to the foreign government official? Why or why not?

8. *The "Little" Tips.* A company's goods have arrived at the port of the host country; but it now seems it is taking a very long time for the goods to clear customs and for the key manager and other company personnel to get their visas approved and other basic government paper work done. The manager's local agent informs him that, yes, indeed, the company will have to wait a long time for these actions to occur unless the manager gives a "little tip" to the lower level government officials involved with the processing of all the paperwork and forms. The local agent suggests about $100 for each official. There are several of them. That is how things are done here, the local agent says; otherwise, the local agent says to be prepared to wait, and wait, and wait. The manager makes the payment of these tips, and the goods and personnel move through customs and immigration promptly. Do you agree with the decision to pay these "tips" to the foreign government officials? Why or why not?

9. *The "Nice" Dinner.* A foreign government official is coming to a company to see a demonstration of its product. The official will make a recommendation as to whether his government should purchase the product. The night before the demonstration day, a key manager of company takes the foreign official and his wife out to a nice dinner, along with manager's spouse and some other company personnel, in order to get acquainted, socialize a little, and explain a bit about the company, the product, and the demonstration. The cost of the dinner, with cocktails and wine, for everyone was about several hundred dollars. The company eventually gets the sale. Do you agree with the decision to take the official and his spouse to dinner? Why or why not?

10. *The Sub-Contract Agreement.* A company is about to secure a major construction contract with a foreign government. The key foreign government official involved in the deal is about to sign the contract and secure the contract with the firm; but first the official requests as a necessary "side-agreement" that the company sub-contract part of the work to a local firm, which "just

happens" to be owned by a cousin of the contractor. The company was in fact contemplating sub-contracting that work; the local company owned by the cousin appears reputable; and the sub-contract price is fair. The general contract with the official's government is a very good one for the company. The company decides to sub-contract the work to contracting firm owned by the cousin. The company gets the general construction contract. Do you agree with the decision to deal with the official's cousin's company? Why or why not?

11. *The Office Lease Agreement.* A company is about to secure a major construction contract with a foreign government. The key foreign government official involved in the deal is about to sign the contract and secure the contract for the firm; but first the official requests as a necessary "side-agreement" that the company rent some office space for the duration of the project in order for the firm's personnel to have a "base of operations" and to supervise the project. The owner of the rental property "just happens" to be a cousin of the official. The company really does not need the office space, as the project will be supervised by its local agents, and consequently the office, which is quite nice, will remain empty most of the time. The rental agreement itself is a reasonable, straightforward, real estate lease agreement. The construction contract between the company and the official's government would be a very good one for the company. The company decides to rent the office space. The company secures the major construction contract. Do you agree with the decision to rent the office space from the official's cousin? Why or why not?

12. *The Disney Trip.* A company is seeking to market its products and services overseas to a large state-controlled company of a foreign government. In order to build "good will," the company intends to pay for the travel, lodging, and entertainment of several hundred foreign company and foreign government officials to Disney World in Orlando, Florida, for a week stay. The company is not located in Orlando, but there will be some brief "seminars" there

about the company; and the foreign government officials eventually will visit company facilities located in another state; nevertheless, the company plans to designate these entire trips as "factory tours." The cost of these trips to the company will be several million dollars; yet if a contract with the state-owned company can be obtained, it will be worth billions of dollars to the firm. The company decides to pay for these trips. The company eventually obtains the contract with the state-owned company. Do you agree with the decision to pay for these "factory tour" trips? Why or why not?

13. *The Charitable Contribution.* In order to finalize a contract between a firm and a foreign government, the key foreign official involved requests that a donation be made by the company of $75,000 to a local charity in the official's home country. The charity is a legitimate one. However, the president of the charity is also the spouse of the foreign official. The company makes the charitable donation. The company gets the contract. Do you agree with this charitable contribution? Why or why not?

14. *The Expense Account Omission.* A company is planning to take a foreign government official out to dinner to discuss business opportunities with the company. The cost of the dinner will be reasonable. The foreign official agrees, but then also requests that her name not be included in any expense account forms of the company for "appearances-sake" in the official's home country. The company agrees to the request. The company ultimately secures some good business deals with the official's government. Do you agree to the company taking the foreign official to dinner under these circumstances? Why or why not?

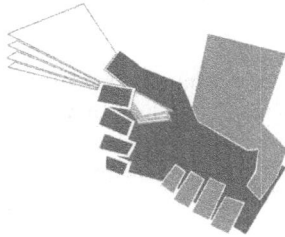

TERMINOLOGY

This section presents a glossary of key or common terms that have been used throughout the work. These terms can serve as a quick reference guide.

- *"Aggressive" or "active" bribery* – a bribe where the bribe-giver desires some type of affirmative action.

- *Anti-bribery Conventions of the Organization for Economic Cooperation and Development* – 1997 and 1998 international treaties prohibiting bribery.

- *"Anything of value"* – FCPA language regarding transfers, encompassing tangible and intangible objects or things, such as the payment of expenses and consulting fees, charitable donations, and offers of employment.

- *Bribe* – the improper payment of money or the improper transfer of something of value in order to unduly influence a decision

- *Bribery* - one form of corruption containing a coercive element; bribery is the granting of some type of benefit in order to unduly influence an action or decision.

- *"Corrupt"* – a requirement for liability pursuant to the FCPA; the payment must be made with the bad intent or improper purpose or "evil mind" to induce the foreign government official to misuse his or her official position and authority in order to wrongfully direct business to one's firm or to obtain some type of undeserved preference or to otherwise accomplish an unlawful end or result.

- **Corruption** - any misuse of entrusted power in the private as well as public sectors.

- **Culture** – the norms, customs, thinking, and manners in which things are done by a group of people in a specific organization, country, or region.

- **Cultural Relativism** – a descriptive theory which merely reports the mores, customs, and conventions of a particular society but makes no moral judgments about those practices.

- **"Defensive" or "passive" bribes** – bribes where the bribe-giver wants something overlooked or protected.

- **"Domestic concerns"** – for FCPA jurisdictional purposes meaning U.S. citizens or residents wherever located as well as any corporation, partnership, organization, including sole proprietorships, that is formed pursuant to the laws of the United States or which have their principal place of business in the United States.

- **Ethical allies** – individuals who refuse to pay bribes and discourage others from expecting kickbacks or giving bribes.

- **Ethical Egoism** – an ethical theory that bases morality on acting to advance one's own self-interest.

- **Ethical Relativism** – an ethical theory that bases morality on what a particular society believes is moral and which sets forth societal conventions as prescriptive moral norms.

- **"Facilitating and expending" payments** – legal payments to foreign officials pursuant to the FCPA; characteristically relatively small payments to lower level government officials to secure the performance of routine government actions

- **Foreign Corrupt Practices Act (FCPA)** - an important 1977 statute in the United States that prohibits U.S. companies from paying or offering to pay anything of value to foreign government officials or employees of state-owned enterprises in order to retain or obtain business or to secure a competitive advantage.

- *"Foreign officials"* - broadly defined pursuant to the FCPA; any person who receives at least a portion of his or her salary from the public treasury of a foreign government will be deemed to be a foreign government official, which includes doctors and nurses who work in state-owned facilities, employees of state-owned companies, as well as government contractors that are working in some type of official government capacity.

- *"Grand" bribes* - where large sums of money typically are given to higher level government officials in order to secure a contract.

- *"Issuers"* – for FCPA jurisdictional purposes encompassing companies that trade their shares on a U.S. stock exchange as well as foreign companies that sell American Depository Receipts on U.S. exchanges.

- *Kantian ethics* – ethical theories and principles of the German philosopher Immanuel Kant which morality on the application of formal ethical test, called the Categorical Imperative, to the action.

- *Opinion Procedure Release process* – a process whereby a firm can submit a set of facts for review by the Department of Justice and receive an opinion as to whether the government would take any enforcement action pursuant to the FCPA based on those facts.

- *"Petty" bribes* - where the sums are smaller, but the payment is usually more frequent, and characteristically involves lower level and local government officials.

- *"Purchase" bribes* – a bribe where the intent is to wrongfully direct business to oneself or one's firm.

- *Transparency International* - a private international anti-corruption and bribery organization which among other functions lists the most corrupt nations in the world based on perceptions of the prevalence of bribery.

- *"Transaction" bribes* – also known as "grease" or "speed money"; payments of relatively small sums to lower level government officials in order to expedite and facilitate access to and performance of routine government services.

- ***Utilitarianism*** – an ethical theory which bases the morality of an action on the production of the greatest amount of good for the greatest number of people; derived from the English Philosopher Jeremy Bentham and John Stuart Mill.

- ***"Variance" bribes*** – a bribe where the corrupt motive is to induce the foreign official to wrongfully exempt one's firm from the host country's law.

- ***Whistleblowing*** – the disclosure of wrongdoing, typically by the employee of a company or organization, to the media and/or the government.

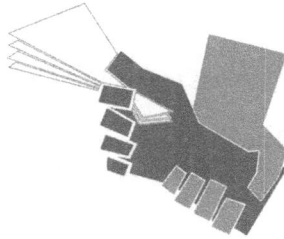

REFERENCES / BIBLIOGRAPHY

Asia-Pacific Human Development Report: Tackling Corruption, Transforming Lives, The Scourge of Corruption (2008). *United Nations Development Program, Chapter 1, pp.17-38.*

Allen, Moira (October 2000). Here Comes the Bribe. *Entrepreneur, p. 48.*

Bishop, Anne W. and Johnson, Brett, W. (February 2009). Ethics Abroad: Minding the Foreign Corrupt Practices Act. *Arizona Attorney, Vol. 45, pp. 24-34.*

Buchan, David (February 8, 1997). French put new take on bribes. *Financial Times, p. 11.*

Byron, Ellen (April 13, 2010). Avon Suspends Executives In Inquiry. *The Wall Street Journal, pp. B1, B4.*

Campbell, R., & Balbach, E. (2009). Building Alliances in Unlikely Places: Progressive Allies and the Tobacco Institute's Coalition Strategy on Cigarette Excise Taxes. *American Journal of Public Health, 99*(7), 1188-1196.

Cavico, Frank J. and Mujtaba, Bahaudin G. (2009). *Business Ethics: The Moral Foundation of Effective Leadership, Management, and Entrepreneurship* (Second Edition). Boston, Massachusetts: Pearson Custom Publishing.

Cavico, Frank J., and Mujtaba, Bahaudin G. (2008). *Legal Challenges for the Global Manager and Entrepreneur.* Dubuque, Iowa: Kendall-Hunt Publishing Company.

Christensen, Dan (November 9, 2008). Oil exec fights bribery lawsuit. *Miami Herald, pp. B1, B2.*

Crawford, David and Searcy, Dionne (April 16, 2010). U.S. Joins H-P Bribery Investigation. *The Wall Street Journal, pp. B1, B5.*

DeGeorge, Richard T. (2006). *Business Ethics* (6th ed.). New Jersey: Pearson-Prentice Hall.

Dickerson, Marla (October 4, 2006). 'Hidden tax' helps stifle Mexico's development. *Sun-Sentinel, p.20A.*

Dworsky, David E. (Spring 2009). Foreign Corrupt Practices Act. *American Criminal Law Review, Vol. 46, pp. 671-707.*

Eaton, Leslie (May 15, 2008). Willbros to Pay $32.3 Million in Bribery Settlement. *The Wall Street Journal, p. B2.*

Emerging-market indicators (October 14, 2006). Bribery. *The Economist, p. 106.*

Esterl, Mike and Crawford, David (December 15, 2008). Siemens to Pay Huge Fine in Bribery Inquiry. *The Wall Street Journal, pp. B1, B5.*

Foreign Corrupt Practices Act of 1977, Public Law No. 95-213, 91 Statutes 1494, 15 United States Code Sections 77, 78; amended by the Foreign Corrupt Practices Act Amendment of 1988, Public Law No. 100-18, 102 Statutes 1107, 1415; and amended by the International Anti-Bribery and Fair Competition Act of 1998, Public Law No. 105-366, 112 Statutes 3302.

Foy, Paul (December 6, 2003). Olympic defendants off the hook. *The Miami Herald, p. 7A.*

Fuhrmans, Vanessa and Catan, Thomas (March 24, 2010). Daimler To Settle With U.S. On Bribes. *The Wall Street Journal, pp. B1, B2.*

Fuhrmans, Vanessa (July 3-5, 2009). Siemens Settles with World Bank on Bribes. *The Wall Street Journal, p. B1.*

Gebauer, M. and Volkery, C. (January 19, 2010). Corruption in Afghanistan: UN Report Claims Bribes Equal to Quarter of GDP. *Spiegel Online.* Retrieved on April 17, 2010 from: http://www.spiegel.de/international/world/0,1518,672828,00.html

Giving Bribes, 2010. *Russian Sign on Punishment of Bribes.* Retrieved on May 04, 2010 from: http://urbanspotlight.wordpress.com/2009/07/15/hello-world/

Gold, Russell (September 4, 2008). Halliburton Ex-official Pleads Guilty in Bribe Case. *The Wall Street Journal, pp. A1, A15.*

Gold, Russell (January 27, 2009). Halliburton to Pay $559 Million To Settle Bribery Investigation. *The Wall Street Journal, p. B3.*

Gold, Russell and Crawford, David (September 12, 2008). U.S., Other Nations Step Up Bribery Battle. *The Wall Street Journal, p. B1.*

Heath, Thomas (July 21, 2000). Ex-Utah Olympic Officials Indicted. *The Washington Post, pp. A1, A10.*

Heilprin, John (March 19, 2010). FBI sting uncovers corruption in the U.N. *Sun-Sentinel, p. 9A.*

Hofstede, G. (1980). *Culture's Consequences: International Differences in Work-related Values.* Beverly Hills, CA: Sage Publications.

Kestenbaum, David (April 29, 2010). Bribery in India: A Good Thing? *National Public Radio,* retrieved April 29, 2010 from: http://www.npr.org/templates/story/story.php?storeyId=126199094.

Kramer, Michael W. (May/June 2002). Corruption and Fraud Stunt Third-world Growth. *The White Paper, Vol. 16, No. 1, pp.23-25.*

Johnstone, Ron (September 2008). The Top 10 Compliance Tips for the Foreign Corrupt Practices Act. *Texas Bar Journal, pp. 643-46.*

Lindsey, Carolyn (2009). More Than You Bargained For: Successor Liability Under the Foreign Corrupt Practices Act. *Ohio Northern University Law Review, Vol. 35, pp. 959-992.*

McFarlin, D. B. and Sweeney, P. D. (2006). *International management: strategic opportunities and cultural challenges* (3rd edition). New York: Houghton Mifflin Company.

Michaels, Daniel and Bryan-Low, Cassell (February 6-7, 2010). BAE to Settle Bribery Cases For More Than $400 Million. *The Wall Street Journal, pp. B1-B6.*

Mitchner, Brandon (April 14, 1997). Germany Says Business Bribes on the Rise. *The Wall Street Journal, p. A1.*

McMahon, Paula (January 20, 2010). 22 charged in bribery scheme. *Sun-Sentinel, p. 3D.*

Mujtaba, B. G. (2010a). *Workplace Diversity Management: Challenges, Competencies and Strategies (2nd edition).* ILEAD Academy Publications; Davie, Florida, United States.

Mujtaba, B. G. (2010b). *Business ethics of retail employees: How ethical are modern workers?* ILEAD Academy Publications; Davie, Florida, United States.

Mujtaba, B. G. (2010c). Bribery, Corruption, and Business Ethics Perceptions of Afghans. *Presentation at the Society of Afghan Engineers Conference.* July 12-15, 2010. Kabul Polytechnic University, Afghanistan.

Mujtaba, B. G. (2010d). Bribery, Narcissism and Anti-Corruption Policies for Promoting a Socially Respo9nsible Business Climate. *Proceedings of 2nd International Conference of South Asia Chapter of AGBA.* July 18-23, 2010. COMSATS Institute of Information Technology. Bhurban, Pakistan.

Mujtaba, B. G. (1996). Ethics and morality in business. *Journal of Global Competitiveness*, 4(1), pp. 339 - 346.

Oppenheimer, Andres (October 3, 2000). IBM executives deny home office knew of bribes. *The Miami Herald, pp. 1E. 12E.*

Pelletier, Kathie L. and Kottke, Janet (2009). Déjà vu All Over Again: Progress and Reversals in Battling Government Corruption. *Journal of Leadership, Accountability and Ethics, Vol. 7(3), pp. 78-93).*

Perez, Evan, and Kendall, Brent (January 20, 2010). Twenty-Two Arrested In U.S. Bribery Probe. *The Wall Street Journal, p. A3.*

Powers, John (January 9, 1999). Olympic-size scandal ousts top organizers. *Sun-Sentinel, pp. 1A, 11A.*

Robertson, Linda (December 15, 1999). IOC ready to offer restructuring. *The Miami Herald, pp. 1D, 2D.*

Robertson, Linda (February 11, 2001) Salt Lake City: Let the 'Games' begin. *The Miami Herald, pp. 1C, 9C.*

Robertson, Linda (February 6, 2002). Can Successful Games squash SLOC scandal? *The Miami Herald, pp. 1D, 6D.*

Rodriguez, Alex (January 20, 2010). U.N.: Corruption a virtual tax on Afghans. *The Miami Herald, p. 15A.*

Rodriguez, Alex (May 1, 2010). Illegal fertilizer supply fuels Afghanistan IEDs. *Sun-Sentinel, p. 19A.*

Rosenberg, Matthew and Zahori, Habid (April 28, 2010). British Man Gets 2 Years for Afghan Bribery. *The Wall Street Journal, p.11A.*

Sanger, David R. (May 24, 1997). 29 Nations Agree to a Bribery Ban. *New York Times, pp.1, 9.*

Sanyal, Rajib E. (2006). *International Management: A Strategic Perspective.* New Jersey: Prentice-Hall.

Searcy, Dionne (December 10, 2009). Small-Scale Bribes Targeted by OECD. *The Wall Street Journal, p. A4.*

Searcy, Dionne (October 8, 2009). To Combat Overseas Bribery, Authorities Make It Personal. *The Wall Street Journal, p. A13.*

Searcy, Dionne (May 20, 2009). U.S. Cracks Down on Corporate Bribes. *The Wall Street Journal, pp. A1, A4.*

Singer, Sam (2009). The Foreign Corrupt Practices Act in the Private Equity Era: Extracting a Hidden Element. *Emory International Law Review, Vol. 23, pp. 273-310.*

Siddiquee, N. A. (June 2010). Combating Corruption and Managing Integrity in Malaysia: A Critical Overview of Recent Strategies and Initiative. *Public Organization Review,* 10(2), 153-171.

Spalding, Andrew Brady (2010). Unwitting Sanctions: Understanding Anti-Bribery Legislation As Economic Sanctions Against Emerging Markets. *Florida Law Review, Vol. 62, pp. 351-397.*

Thomas, Cortney C. (2010). The Foreign Corrupt Practices Act: A Decade of Rapid Expansion Explained, Defended, and Justified. *The University of Texas School of Law The Review of Litigation, Vol. 29, pp. 439-462.*

Timberg, Craig (May 8, 2005). Normally rampant, bribery suddenly taboo. *Miami Herald, p. 27A.*

Transparency International, 2009. *Corruption Perception Index Data for 2009.* Retrieved on April 20, 2010 from: http://transparency.org/policy_research/surveys_indices/cpi/2009.

UNODC, 2010. *Corruption in Afghanistan: Bribery as reported by the victims.* United Nations Office of Drugs and Crime Report. Retrieved on April 17, 2010 from: http://viewer.zmags.com/publication/8515c039#/8515c039/1

Weinograd, Charles B. (2010). Clarifying Grease: Mitigating the Threat of Overdeterrence by Defining the Scope of the Routine Governmental Action Exception. *Virginia Journal of International Law, Vol. 50, pp. 509-549.*

Yost, Pete and Barrett, Delvin (April 2, 2010). $185M Daimler bribery settlement OK'd. *The Miami Herald, p. 2C.*

Walker, Marcus (April 16, 2010). Tragic Flaw: Graft Feeds Greek Crisis. *The Wall Street Journal, pp. A1, A15.*

Zamiska, Nicholas, Leow, Jason, and Oser, Shai (May 30, 2007). China Confronts Crisis Over Food Safety. *The Wall Street Journal, p. A3.*

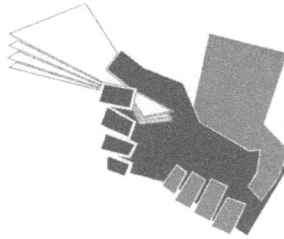

INDEX

Author Biographies

Frank J. Cavico, J.D., is a professor of Business Law and Ethics at the H. Wayne Huizenga School of Business and Entrepreneurship of Nova Southeastern University. He teaches primarily in the MBA program. He was the creator of the core MBA course, The Values of Legality, Morality, and Social Responsibility in Business. In 2000, he was awarded the Excellence in Teaching Award by the Huizenga School. In 2006, he was honored as Professor of the Year by the Huizenga School. Professor Cavico holds a J.D. degree from St. Mary's University School of Law and a B.A. from Gettysburg College. He also possesses a Master of Laws degree from the University of San Diego - School of Law and a Master's degree in Political Science from Drew University. Professor Cavico is licensed to practice law in the states of Florida and Texas. He has worked as a federal government regulatory attorney and as counsel for a labor union; and has practiced general civil law and immigration law in South Florida. He has published five books and numerous law review articles and management journal works. Frank can be reached at: cavico@nova.edu.

Bahaudin G. Mujtaba, D.B.A., is an Associate Professor of Management and Human Resources at Nova Southeastern University's H. Wayne Huizenga School of Business and Entrepreneurship. During the past twenty-five years, Bahaudin has served as manager, trainer, and management development specialist in the corporate world as well as a director, department chair and faculty member in academia. He has authored over sixteen books and nearly one-hundred journal articles. Bahaudin has also presented and lectured in academic and professional conferences in many countries across the globe during the last few decades. His areas of research are ethics, higher education, leadership, faculty training, and cross-cultural management. Bahaudin can be reached at: mujtaba@nova.edu.

www.ingramcontent.com/pod-product-compliance
Lightning Source LLC
Chambersburg PA
CBHW031947190326
41519CB00007B/696